THE
GRAVEYARD
WANDERERS

Folk Necromancy in Transmission, Volume 7

Series editors: Dr Alexander Cummins and
             Jesse Hathaway Diaz

OTHER TITLES IN THE SERIES:

Cypriana: Old World, edited by Alexander Cummins, Jesse Hathaway Diaz, and Jennifer Zahrt

The Immaterial Book of Saint Cyprian, by José Leitão

A Book of the Magi, by Dr. Alexander Cummins

Svartkonstböcker: A Compendium of the Swedish Black Art Book Tradition by Dr. Thomas K. Johnson

The Way of the Living Ghost by John Anderson

Opening the Vermillion Spirit by John Anderson

The Graveyard Wanderers

The Wise Ones
+
*The Dead
in Sweden*

Dr Thomas K. Johnson

Revelore Press
Olympia WA
MMXXII

THE GRAVEYARD WANDERERS: THE WISE ONES
+ THE DEAD IN SWEDEN

© 2022 The Estate of Dr Thomas K. Johnson

Seventh volume of the Folk Necromancy in Transmission series conceived and curated by Dr Alexander Cummins and Jesse Hathaway Diaz.

THE GRAVEYARD WANDERERS first appeared in 2012 in a limited hardback, fine-bound edition restricted to 180 copies through The Society for Esoteric Endeavour, based in the United Kingdom. What you hold in your hands is the second edition, printed in paperback, for the nomadic necromancer.

All rights reserved. No part of this publication may be reproduced or utilized in any form or by any means, electronic or mechanical, including photocopying, recording, or by any information storage and retrieval system, without permission in writing from the Publishers.

Book and cover design by Joseph Uccello.
Cover art © 2022 K Lenore Siner.

ISBN 978-1-947544-39-0

Revelore Press
1910 4th Ave E PMB141
Olympia, WA 98506
United States

www.revelore.press

Contents

Foreword to this Edition by Michael Tarplee	7
Prologue to the First Edition by Ben Fernee	9
Prologue to the Second Edition by Dr Alexander Cummins	12
Initiation	16
Healing with the Dead	28
The Detection & Transfixation of Thieves	38
The Dead Control Animals & People	49
Hexing with the Dead	56
The Dead Give Protection	67
Winning with the Dead	75
Shooting with the Dead	79
Invisibility	84
The Spiritus	88
The Rune-Stone	93
The Ring-Belt	99
Some Warnings	105
Afterword: The Wise & Their World by Dr Thomas K. Johnson	107
References	120
Select Bibliography	136

Foreword to this Edition

THIS book is the second edition of Dr. Tom Johnson's first published work and is a compilation of the rites of the Wise Ones of Sweden concerning the Dead. It is named after the specialists who would visit graveyards seeking magical power from the artifacts of the dead. They would gather bones, graveyard dirt, coffin nails, shroud needles and such to craft their spells.

Graveyard Wanderers was to be the first in a series, each focusing on a particular aspect of the Wise Ones' craft. Dr. Johnson chose the ancestors as the topic of this first book to honor their primary importance in the passing of such lore. Such a series of compilations would have made it easier to survey the many spells covered in his dissertation to find a particular topic. As it was, Dr. Johnson joined the spirits of his ancestors before his vision for this series could be completed. As Dr. Johnson's husband and partner of over twenty years, I was blessed to receive his insights into this material as he researched and wrote his dissertation.

In this book, one will find methods to commence dealings with the spirits of the dead. After rendering payment for use of their artifacts, the items could be used to effect healing, hexing, protection, and assistance. The powers of the dead infused the artifacts and rendered them potent. It was believed that the realm of the dead shared a border with the realm of the gods, and thus the dead were particularly effective in appealing to the powers of nature.

In addition to the actual spells of the Graveyard Wanderers, this book contains Dr. Johnson's notes concerning the spells. It ends with a section on the overall viewpoint of the Wise Ones, their approaches to magic and their techniques utilizing the invisible powers of nature. Such books were often credited with magical power themselves simply by the nature of their contents. They were more than mere textbooks, but allies themselves in the practice of the Dark Art. Perhaps you will find this book to be such an ally.

Michael Tarplee
MMXXII

Prologue to the First Edition

HEREIN is examined one aspect of the practice of the Wise Ones of Sweden; their relationship with the Dead. Of this, it has been said:

Hardly any magical item has been so much used by the Wise Ones as graveyard earth and human bone, and in certain cases coffin nails, fragments from the headstone and such like from the cemetery. This was illustrated by the title "graveyard-wanderer" that was given to the Wise Ones. "He was a real graveyard man," it was said of a wise man in Holm, Medelpad.[1]

The method by which a wise person received a special ability might also be captured in the word used to refer to them. "Graveyard wanderer" (Sw. kyrkogdårdsgdångare) refers to the common visitation of the wise folk to cemeteries to procure human skeletal remains or "graveyard earth" (Sw. kyrkogårdsmull) for use in magical rites, and to the practice of enlisting the aid of ancestral spirits. The following excerpt about Kristina i Prekebo, known locally as "Prekeborskan," and her errands in grave- yards, is exemplary: once she had been all the way down to Halmstad. There was a farmhand who was to convey her home by horse. But it was the worst trip he'd ever been on, he said, because at every cemetery they drove past that night she wanted to go and talk to the dead, as well as fetch some earth from the graves that she could then use as medicine.[2]

Whoever wants to learn to do magic should fetch a bone from the cemetery. After that, it will be possible to see and know more than others.[3]

There now follows the rituals and teachings of the Wise Ones, largely as written by themselves in their Black Art Books and in accounts they recorded of their practice. The nature of this tradition is startling.

Both men and women became Graveyard Wanderers. Though the path was solitary, they were keenly interested in the activities of other practitioners; who might be regarded as enemies or vital sources of lore. Though some may see survivals of Catholicism and even Paganism in their practice, the religion of the Wise Ones was, broadly, that of their neighbours, Protestant Christianity. However, an occasional phrase signals a more manipulative than supplicatory regard for the Holy Trinity than would be expected of good Christians. Whilst some Wise Ones asserted that they maintained the healing mission of Jesus on Earth, their path seems essentially amoral. Healing and hexing, killing and curing, were regarded as two sides of the same coin. Here, we concentrate upon their practice in relation to the powers of death, and their dealings with the spirits of the Dead.

Some comment, printed in grey,† has been given and, for this, the present writer must plead guilty. I will also ask for the endnotes to be taken into consideration but note that, occasionally, some mitigating circumstances occur; such as when I successfully repeat information supplied by Dr. Johnson. It is he who translated these rituals, charms, and accounts. His labour is our debt. One cannot imagine the Gordion knot of obscure dialects and archaic handwriting that required untangling. More than communicating the sense, Dr. Johnson has brought to the English reader the austere elegance of that poetry of word and deed that is preserved in these spells. And the deeds done were truly shocking; therein lies their power. Occult tradition affirms that an act of transgression can make a magical working effective.

Having learnt of the Graveyard Wanderers, the natural response is to desire knowledge of the context of their practice. Dr. Johnson comes to our rescue and amply satisfies such understandable cravings with the *Wise & Their World*, the text that concludes this book.

Ben Fernee
MMXII

---

† Publisher's note: In this edition, these comments appear in a **different font**.

Prologue to the Second Edition

*G*RAVEYARD *Wanderers* is a collection that haunts about a particular necromantic folk magic: of seeking empowerment, healing, justice, and even tuition from (ghost-wrangling) ghosts and the folk relics of borrowed churchyard remains. As a historical primer on nigromantic cunning it further explicates nuanced relationships between the living and the dead throughout time and custom. Anthologised together in a single collected volume, these workings begin to enrich an understanding and engagement with their shared craft logics and recurring motifs; numbers, directions, days, and all the other minutiae of practical sorcery.

For it is (*inter alia*) works done on Thursdays, works of requisitioning and returning churchyard finger-bones, of laying coins, and marking earth-fast stones and their secrets; of cedar chips and shroud-stitched sewing needles. It may be the actions performed thrice: from crossing oneself three times to chipping a trio of splinters from a place of power. Those versed in English cunning may recognise certain familiar techniques in our Scandinavian cousins' wise ways: a hazel wand for circling a grave, skull-moss salves, and countless works of bread and bone. These are also works that highlight—*one way or another*—respect for those departed workers who were already haunting graveyards in life. Necromancy is always ancestral, and always a matter of both the departed and the remaining.

The first edition of *Graveyard Wanderers* was published before Dr. Johnson's more extensive translations, surveys, and analyses were committed to print as *Svartkonstböcker: A Compendium of the Swedish Black Art Book Tradition* (Revelore, 2019). Having worked on the latter collection as part of the Folk Necromancy in Transmission team, my fellow editors and I felt it useful to include additional citations and pagination from their original manuscript transcriptions and translations now published in *Svartkonstböcker* for the necromantic operations collected in this second edition of *Wanderers*. One can thus cross-reference from this nigromantic anthology to the sources and supporting material more easily. We hope these supplementary endnotes aid both students and practitioners in sourcing deeper contexts for manuscript analysis and further lines of historical inquiry to illuminate these folk magics.

In framing how this collection may thus best help you as a practitioner and/or scholar, you may ask yourself two questions as you analyse the workings and operations assembled herein. Firstly, consider theory, methodology, cosmo-vision and all and ask *how does it work?* Secondly, consider purpose: *what is it for?*

To start you on the first question, we should note whether dangerous "mischief with corpses" or seeking aid from the inhabitants of the kingdom of death, we may observe manipulation of contagions of power and affect, control over natural forces and agents, and seeking and apprehending (respectfully and otherwise) the aid of the flora and fauna of the graveyard. We can note transference of disease *away to* the land of the dead by their borrowed bones; but we can also detect empowerments *received from* the souls of the churchyard through their anonymised relics and in other manners.

The purpose of these workings should remind us that they were—and continue to be—used *by* folk *for* folk. Specifically, they are for helping folk in perceiving, calling, and bargaining with the dead for their aid and support in both mundane and so-called supernatural matters. Such wise wanderers' work may include formal sorcerous approaches of 'selling oneself into the power of the Invisibles'; but these workings themselves are for easing the very real and particular pains and distresses of the living, from everyday tooth ache to serious illness and chronic malady. These efforts to cohere and direct the sorcerous possibilities of the Kingdom of the Dead spring from human needs. Ideally they return the living to their proper places and functioning along with the leased *materia* of the dead to theirs.

Having considered of the purposes of these operations it is fitting we conclude by considering the purpose of this second edition of this collection of nigromantic operations. It is our hope by bringing forth these respectfully borrowed bones of wise workings, attitudes, customs, observances, and spellcrafts that Dr. Johnson's work may continue to inspire and re-call those who continue the wanderings amongst the dead on behalf of the living.

Dr. Alexander Cummins
MMXXII

¶ Initiation

*One's introduction to the Dead
so as to receive insight
and acquire their services.*

Thus, may one become a sorcerer.

To Gain Sight[4]

Go to a churchyard. Recite this over a gravestone whilst crossing yourself:

> *Your Sight shall be in my Sight*
> *in whose name you rest here*
> *I will not disturb you*
> *but hoped that you*
> *in the name of peace may sleep*
> *so that I may see the Hidden*
> *and see its power*
> *hear its celebration*
> *and help in need.*
>
> *Could you*
> *O Holy Ghost*
> *give to me of your power*
> *in the name of the Holy Crucified One*
> *Amen.*

Then make crosses over your eyes, three times, over each lid.

This ritual reflects the benevolent aspect of the Wise Ones. The Christian Holy Ghost (unusually, not the Holy Trinity) is requested to enable sight of the "Hidden" (i.e., the Kingdom of the Dead), to hear its celebrations and realise its potential to help the living.

A Flute[5]

A bone flute from the churchyard, or made from a tree branch found there; to blow the spirit through.

In Britain, the use of such flutes has been associated with the Ancient Order of Bonesmen.

To Know the Invisible Sciences[6]

If one wants to know about the sciences of the Invisibles—their wisdom—namely about the families of Wights and Lucifers, then one goes to a grave on a Thursday night between the hours of twelve and one o'clock.

One takes a little earth from the grave, cuts the left ring finger, so that three drops of blood fall down on the grave-earth and then throw the earth on you as the priest does when he casts the earth onto a coffin.

When one has done so, one has sold oneself into the power of the Invisibles, and then you can learn from them anything one desires to learn in this way.

It will become clear that Thursday night was the preferred time for graveyard wandering, and graveyard earth was a crucial tool of the craft. Here, by making himself one with the Dead, the practitioner acquires the power to communicate with other families of spirits as well, and may gain knowledge from them. This ritual has no Christian component, the Wise One simply places himself under the power of the Invisibles.

Charm to Borrow a Human Bone[7]

> *Får jag låna ditt lilla ben,*
> *om en ... ska du få det igen!*
>
> *If I can borrow your little bone,*
> *then in a week* you will get it back again!*

*Or day, month, or year, &c.—the required time period is stated. The Graveyard Wanderers removed bones from the churchyard, but they were borrowed, and had to be returned.

To Become a Sorcerer[8]

If one wishes to become a true sorcerer, but without having to sell oneself to the Devil, then one should go to the churchyard on a Thursday night between two and four o'clock. This is what one says:

> *Inhabitants of the Kingdom of Death*
> *this payment I borrow from you*
> *that sometime you might tell me*
> *how to find out that which I wish to know.*

Then one goes up to the church-bell and scrapes a little metal from it and keeps it in a bottle. If one then wants to find out about something, whatever it may be, then one goes to the churchyard on a Thursday night and says:

> *Inhabitants of the Kingdom of Death.*
> *Come forth!*
> *Tell me how I should restore this coin that I*
> *   have borrowed from you*
> *it shall be paid back to you on that day that*
> *   I enter with you into eternity.*

Then one may learn from the spirits anything that one wishes to know, even if there is no earthly way for you to discover it. Each time one wants to find out about something, then one goes to the churchyard and repeats the ritual.

The Wise One purloins some bell metal (apparently considered to be akin to a coin) and promises to return it when he joins them in the Kingdom of Death. In exchange for this undertaking he requests knowledge. There is no Christian component to this ritual, simply a rather manipulative contract between the Wise One and the Dead. Also, there is no infernal aspect; the services of the Dead being obtained *instead* of selling oneself to the Devil.

To Conjure a Dead Person from the Earth[9]

If you wish to do mischief with a corpse, then take a little earth from a grave in the churchyard. Tie it into a piece of cloth with a long thread attached. Then go into the air above where the Dead One's body lies. Bore a hole and tie a knot onto the corpse's chest. Haul up the knot very slowly, then the corpse will rise. Do it several times, raising and lowering the corpse again.

However, if you want to conjure a dead mother or father, or whatever relative you choose, even if they have lain in the earth for twenty years, then you go out in the evening, out through your door and take a bit of chalk and write the Dead One's baptismal and common name over the door, as well as over all the other doors that enter the house.

Then put a penknife between the names over each door and then the Latin with Hebrew:

Comotote Prili Sali.

Two hours thereafter the Dead One will come and place themselves inside the door of the house. But no one should speak to them. And when the dead one has stayed a little while, then you go out and take the penknife out and strike out the Latin and Hebrew.

Then you go inside and cast seeds and quicksilver all over the dead one, remaining silent. Then the dead one will depart.

The instruction to "Go into the air above where the dead one's corpse lies" probably infers that the Wise One is to be strung from ropes tied to convenient trees, or perhaps constructs a suitable improvised timber structure.

To See and Speak with Invisible Spirits[10]

To reveal invisible spirits and to be able to hear and speak with them, in whatever way one desires, so as to find out hidden things write your name and then these words in red letters on a chip of spruce wood:

> *Filx Gackte ol hordea*
> *OSS.YQQ Pelock Bjelsebubb*
> *Behov vara*

On a Thursday evening go to the cemetery and put that chip under an earth-fast stone. Return there the following Thursday evening. Then take the chip and say, giving their names:

> *I order you spirits*
> *to come and meet me here next Thursday*
>   *evening*
> *in the name of*
> *Domine Pater Filius Sancti Spiritus*
> *or in the name of*
> *God the Father*
> *and of the Son*
> *and of the Holy Spirit.*

Then, go thence the third Thursday evening, then the chip will be gone, and a little round stone will be in its place. Take this stone and keep it, then the spirits will come to you, and then you can get to know whatever you ask of them; but don't ask too much all at once, because then they get too tired, save it for later.

When you have the stone in your pocket, you will never lack for money. Take the stone in a bottle and knock it once, for each spirit you want to speak with. They shall procure for you in this way whatever you require, from wherever in the whole world.

To Obtain Three Secret Words[11]

Take a one-year-old hazel branch and make a circle around the grave. With your left hand, take up earth from the grave three times. Say this:

> *I conjure you*
> *you skeleton and your spirit*
> *by Christ*
> *by the Virgin Mary's birth*
> *and the earthly path of the holy evangelists*
>   *and apostles*
> *that you rise up and meet me here at this*
>   *place*
> *before the hour of twelve*
> *when I shall ask you secretly*
> *and you shall answer me three words*
> *which I shall not reveal*
> *and I conjure you that you will not go*
>   *outside this circle*
> *nor harm a hair upon my head*
> *in the name of the Holy Trinity*

*and of Mary's birth
and the earthly path of the holy evangelists
 and the apostles.
Amen.*

Write then these signs around the circle:

Then plant the branch into the earth and step backwards from the circle.

When the spirit finishes speaking with you, he will run widdershins around the circle. As he runs nine circuits, you throw the graveyard earth over him three times, and he will immediately sink into the ground.

To Obtain the Service of a Spirit[12]

Write the following with your own blood, upon a small piece of paper:

*I give you this as a proof
you impure spirit.*

And sign your name.

On a Thursday, go back to the church making sure that no one catches up with you, or meets you. Put the piece of paper under the threshold of the church door.

On the following Thursday grasp the lock of the church door. Say:

> *I give you this as a proof*
> *you impure spirit*
> *so that you will meet me*
> *on the next Thursday evening.*

Then go home again, but be careful that no one catches up with you, or meets you, for you must be all by yourself. Then go back the third Thursday evening just as day gives way to night. You will find your note has gone. Stay there, at that place, until a spirit comes forth and gives you a box. He will then go his way, but you must not be frightened, for he will say nothing to you. In the box is a little bell. When you ring that little bell, then the spirit will come forth to you, and will be visible to your eyes but not to anyone else's. This spirit must serve you and do what you command him to, whether for ill or good, and he must procure for you everything that you desire of him, whether money or other goods, or even other arts that you wish to try. But as often as you want him to serve you, then you have to ring the bell, and then he will come forth to do what you command him.

Procuring the Service of a Dead Person[13]

The Sámi Adolf said to take three hairs from a corpse, then say:

> *You who rest here*
> *in whose name you now sleep*
> *with this you shall give to me power to hear*

> *what I wish*
> *you shall only follow me*
> *you are the servant of my spirit*
> *in the name of all the Saints*
> *until the beginning of Judgment Day.*

Recite aloud at 12 o'clock at night.
 Cross then +++ times over the coffin.

Usually, the Wise One sought the service of a spirit until a bone was returned, or perhaps until the practitioner passed from the Land of the Living into the Kingdom of Death. Here, however, the spirit must serve the Wise One long after his death, until the morning of Judgment Day.

¶ Healing with the Dead

*Whereby the Dead
now beyond suffering
take pain from the living.*

The Head Nail[14]

One might also take body parts of the newly departed to perform magic with: especially of suicides and the executed. Gallows nails were magically effective. Especially the "head nail" with which the head of the condemned had been fastened to the pole. One could heal illness in both humans and animals with this.

For Prognosis[15]

Bones of the Dead and graveyard earth were of great use to the Wise One. If he wanted to find out the prognosis for a sick person, he would take a piece of bread in one hand and a dead man's bone in the other, but secretly, so no one could see what he had. Then, when he went in to the sick one, he let the patient make a choice. If they chose the bread, he would get better. But if he chose the bone, he would die.

To Aid Deformity[16]

Go early to the churchyard and borrow a corpse bone and soak it in the dew. Then stroke with it over the affected limb. It will also help with injuries. It is done in the new and waning moons to help women. Then the bone is put back in the same place, and earth is thrown over it. Say:

> *Let my weakness now rot away*
> *with you in the earth*
> *as this bone does.*

Telling a Spirit to Accept an Incurable Illness[17]

If a person has not healed, even if they have sought out all the cunning folk and even the doctors, then on a Thursday night – best during the waning moon – go to a grave and have with you a piece of cloth that belongs to the invalid. Take the cloth and wrap it widdershins around the gravestone. Tie a knot and say:

> *You N.N.*
> *who lie here*
> *you know nothing.*

Then make another knot and say:

> *You can take this sickness from N.N.*

For the third time, tie a knot while you say:

> *For you feel nothing*
> *in the name of God the Father*
> *and of the Son*
> *and of the Holy Ghost.*

The sick one should then keep the piece of cloth, and untie all three knots, then he, or she, will be healthy.

To Ease Pain[18]

Say three times:

> *Your pain shall fade*
> *as a dead person that is in the earth does*
> *in the name of the Father*
> *the Son*
> *and the Holy Ghost.*

To Aid in Cases of Deformity[19]

A way to help, without fail, all people's deformities is as follows. Each must do this for him or herself. If their parents have died, go to a churchyard in the summertime, when there is a lot of dew and the graves are open. Take a corpse's bone and put it to the side of the churchyard. But remember, the bone that is borrowed should accord with the limb that is afflicted. Go to the churchyard early in the new and waning moon. Dip this bone in the dew, and stroke it upon your injuries, it will surely help. For another kind this is done during the quarter to full moon. When one has finished using it, put the bone back in the same place, and cover it with earth, as you throw on the earth say:

> *Let now my weakness*
> *which this bone now owns*
> *rot with you in the earth.*

Calling for Assistance[20]

Go to a grave, pull up a plant with its roots. Say this while you take it:

> *When I take you*
> *the one who lies in this grave,*
> *do not deny me this root*
> *that I take for plentiful blessings*
> *rather give me your power and blessing*
> *rest soundly in your grave*
> *I wish you no ill.*
> *Work peacefully in God's name.*

Afterwards, keep the root indoors.

This ritual shows that the Wise Ones could be respectful to the spirits of the Dead.

To Aid Backache[21]

This is a good remedy for those suffering badly with lumbago.

Go to the cemetery and find a newly opened grave, look for where the earth has mixed with the remains of a dead body. Take a water vessel full of this earth as a loan, and leave a one-crown coin in the grave. Then go from there in silence.

Upon returning home, empty the vessel in a bathtub or such and fill the tub with water. All this takes place on a Thursday night. In the morning remove all the dirt from the bathtub, whereupon the sick one is bathed completely in the water. And however difficult the sickness may be, it will disappear completely through this cure.

But you should take the dirt back to the graveyard and take back the coin.

With graveyard earth, both when helping another, or when overcoming them, every time one borrows from the graveyard one should have serious intent, and keep in mind what you desire. Then, it will come to pass; whether for good or for ill.

To Heal Painful Bones[22]

For very painful or, so-called, inflamed bones take a human bone and put it in the gap in the fuel that one makes when starting a fire in the oven. Burn it and then remove it and grind it completely into a fine powder. Sift this together with flour, and then spread it on the affected part. Be very careful when using it, not to get any in the eyes. It will make you blind without any hope of regaining your sight. It is very dangerous, but in cases of great need, very useful.

To Get Rid Of Worms[23]

Take some worms from each tree and go to the churchyard on a Thursday morning before the sun comes up. Do not look behind you as you travel there. Drop the worms into an open grave; if you cannot find one, make a hole in a closed grave with a staff. This should be done in silence. Then think, or say:

> *Hence will all worms go*
> *that are in N.N. garden*
> *in the name of God the Father*
> *the Son*
> *and the Holy Ghost.*

Then leave the churchyard and go back to the garden again. Do not look behind you as you go. Find a tree that is in the middle of the garden and place in its freshest foliage a needle threaded with yarn that has been used previously to sew through a shroud that a corpse has been wrapped in, though washed three times.

To Cure Flen[24]

Recite the following words three times and the third time draw a five-pointed star over the affected area:

> *Flennar flena opos.*
> *Flen you shall shrink, be subdued,*
> *[the person's name & their father's name]*
> *as a dead man under the ground*
> *far away in the woods*
> *in the name of the Father*
> *and of the Son*
> *and of the Holy Spirit.*

All Types of Remedies Useful for Many Circumstances[25]

Take the moss that grows on a dead man's skull, peat pellets, a bell that is found in a flowing stream, and earth that is dug up in a left shoe whilst the priest buries a body. This is obtained in the following way; when the priest says in the name of the Father and of the Son and of the Holy Spirit, each time one takes up some earth with the leather from the left shoe. Also, take the remains of homespun wool that has lain in the earth, snakeskin that lies at a crossroads, a wedding ring, asafoetida, garlic, castoreum, valerium, the roots of rushes, three drops of blood from a bat, nails from a corpse's hand, or its nameless finger, as well as a cuckoo's left claw.

To Dull Pain[26]

> *Jesus, he walked into the churchyard.*
> *There he sought the means*
> *and there he healed wounds*
> *and dulled pain*
> *and you will fall asleep*
> *and the pain will dull*
> *and this in the name of the Triune God.*
> *Amen.*

A Cure for Stroke[27]

Take peas so that they sprout, and put them aside. Take a human skull from whom the stroke seems to come. Then the mother will pee three drops each morning into it, and, in silence, give it to the child to drink on an empty stomach for nine mornings in a row. If you forget, then you need to start over again, and if you haven't a skull, then she can pee into her right hand and give it to her child.

¶ The Detection & Transfixation of Thieves

The Dead send dreams that reveal the thief.

*In return for coin
or the promise of peaceful rest
the Dead can torment thieves
or transfix them
communicating the stillness of Death
until the Wise One commands their release.*

*But the Wise One may not punish
a miscreant thus constrained.*

Transfixation of Thieves & Finding Stolen Goods[28]

If you wore a human bone on a string around the neck, one could transfix thieves even before they left the scene of their crime, and they couldn't move again until the Wise One released them. If you took a human bone, sawed it in half and laid the pieces in a cross under one's pillow, then during the night you would have a dream of where the thief was, and also the location of the stolen goods.

To See a Thief[29]

Take a human bone from the churchyard
    and a little splinter from under the altar
    and a little cloth from the pulpit
    and a little fragment from the church door.

Put these under your head at night with these words written down, and with the desire in your mind wrap them in a linen cloth:

> *To get to see the thief.*

Then you will see him.

Another. Take raven's feathers, namely the middle and topmost feathers from the left wing, and put them under your head at night, and when you sleep then you will see the form of the thief as the feathers turn together in a ring.

Detection of a Thief[30]

To see the thief in your sleep. Dig up a human bone. Put it under your pillow when you sleep. Then you will see the thief.

To Show a Thief in a Glass of Water and Protect One's Property[31]

It works like this, you go to the cemetery and get ahold of a skeleton that has not been destroyed by the teeth of time. From this you take the longest finger of the left hand and leave a one-crown piece in payment for it. While doing this say:

> *Thou dead*
> *this, I borrow from you*
> *so that you will help me*
> *when I call upon you*
> *to show who the thief is*
> *and to return the stolen goods.*

If you want yet another wish, you can state it, since you have three wishes—but no more. This experiment you should do alone on a Thursday night between twelve and one o'clock. Now if someone has been robbed and you want to show him who the thief is, then you stir the liquor in a glass three times widdershins with the finger of the dead person. Then the thief will become visible, so that anyone can see him. If you want to have the stolen goods returned, order the spirit of the finger to do so.

I heard last winter of one place where, during a wedding, one of the guests made off with a gold watch. Because there was a Wise One among the wedding guests, who knew the art of showing the thief and getting stolen goods returned, the victim wanted to get the watch back again. This the sorcerer promised; and in an hour's time one of the neighbours came running up, as if for his life, with the watch in his hand and returned it to the owner.

The thief said that when he had come home with the stolen watch and gone to bed, he was surrounded by a group of spirits who ordered him to return the stolen goods; if he didn't obey, they said they would take him with them to Eternity. This terrified the thief so much that he didn't even have time to put on more than a pair of trousers before he rushed back to return the watch.

The owner of the watch said, though, that had he known just who the thief was, then for all the world, he would not have wished him exposed to all the people there.

If you want to protect your possessions, for example things that are left out under the open sky, and you own such an amulet, then you go three times widdershins around them. Then, if a thief comes along and grasps something, he will remain standing and will not be able to move from that spot until the owner returns. To release the thief, you say:

> *Thanks shall you have*
> *you who have stood here*
> *and guarded my possessions.*

Then the thief will be released from his enchantment. But if the owner is angry and becomes abusive, then he can expect other after-effects, which can destroy him for his entire life.

To Transfix Thieves[32]

Take a woollen yarn in a needle that has been threaded widdershins. Go to a corpse and pass the thread through the left hand and go three times around the grave widdershins and put the needle and the thread in the grave.

To Transfix Thieves[33]

When a corpse is being enshrouded, speak to the one who sews so as to obtain the needle and thread, but it must be the same as was actually used, and no other. And when you get hold of a grass snake, take him living and unharmed, and put him in front of your possessions upon an earth-fast stone until he dries up, and take his head off him, and stick the needle through and let it remain there on the thread, and thread it through that which you wish to keep safe.

Snakes were important to the Wise Ones, being both infernal pestilence incarnate, but also a source of power. An earth-fast stone is, presumably, protruding bedrock and is often utilised in Black Art Book practice.

A Spirit to Protect One's Property[34]

Go to the churchyard, dig up a human bone and ask to borrow it for however long a time, and say:

> *I exorcise you*
> *you spirit of the bone*
> *by the Virgin Mary's birth*
> *and by all the Apostles' paths*
> *and I wake you up*
> *to become a guardian over everything I own*
> *so that no thief*
> *whoever it might be*
> *will be able to steal any of my goods*
> *but will rather remain standing in place*
> *until I allow my guardian to release him.*

As long as you have the bone under lock and key, the spirit of the bone will be a watchful guardian over your house.

To Restore Stolen Goods[35]

Talk to someone who is to enshroud a corpse and obtain the needle with five quarters [a measure] of thread that has been used to sew up the shroud. Keep this needle and thread and take the following:

Three pinecone scales, and take them apart and cut them up finely. Remove the seedpods from the seeds.

A knife's measure of water from three springs that run into the same stream

Nine grains of salt

Three drops of blood out of the left ring finger

Three pinches of flour

And recite the Our Father, and the Lord's Benediction and say:

> *As truly as you are a thief in the world*
> *just as truly you will come back over*
> *mountains and valleys*

Then draw this figure on wood:

Then get seven button-holes and blow the mixture through them without seeing where it goes.

To Transfix Thieves when They are About to Steal[36]

Take a human skull from the churchyard and borrow it for a certain period of time, and make sure that when that time has passed you bring it back again. Borrow the skull in the name of the Holy Trinity; and at the same time state what use you will make of it. With this skull go three times around your property, and each time recite the Our Father. When you now come to the place you started, say:

> *As still as this corpse lies*
> *that's as still as you will remain*
> *you thief*
> *who invites himself in to steal*
> *remain here inside this place*
> *that I have encircled*
> *until I myself come to you*
> *and give you permission to leave.*

Then bury the skull and recite the Our Father.

To Restore that which has Been Stolen[37]

Cut away for yourself three chips or bits from that place that you know the thing was taken from. Take them to church and put them under the altar. Leave them there for three Thursday evenings. Then pass them three times around your right thigh, and lastly put them in a grave or a coffin.

To Force a Thief to Confess[38]

You take something that you believe belongs to the thief. On a Thursday, having fasted, go to the churchyard and bury that item under a gravestone. Then say:

> *I conjure you*
> *you spirit of the dead one's body*
> *that you will drive N.N.*
> *the damned thief that stole from me*
> *so that he confesses this publicly*
> *or returns the goods*
> *or pain and suffering to him*
> *until I shall order you otherwise*
> *in the name of the Father*
> *of the Son*
> *And the Holy Ghost.*

To Transfix a Thief upon the Spot[39]

You borrow a bone from the churchyard at a certain time. Then you go around the place three times widdershins and say:

> *Stand still*
> *like that state in which this body lies*
> *so still you shall stand*
> *until I come.*

When you begin to walk, when you've made it through the place, then write these words on the top of the bone:

> *I.N.R.I.*

Then bury this bone again in its place.

To Transfix a Thief[40]

Leave home silently, and go to the churchyard, taking care that no one should meet or greet you either on the way there, or when you go home. When you have got there and found the human skull you seek, say:

> *I, N.N.*
> *pray to you for forgiveness*
> *for taking you*
> *for such a long time*
> *so that you will guard me, and mine from*
>   *thieves.*
> *When the time is up*
> *I shall with reverence*
> *bring you back*
> *and bury you.*

In just this way he should be brought back silently and be buried, but then you may talk to whomever you want. When you have the skull with you, put it in a leather bag with a piece of a chasuble and a communion wafer in a secret place. You may not speak harshly to the thief thus caught.

¶ The Dead Control Animals & People

The stillness of Death is communicated to:

>*human*
>*beast*
>*bird*
>*& fish.*

Even fire may be halted!

To Control Animals and Fire[41]

Take earth from three graveyards and place it under the church altar for three Sundays. Then put it in your shoes under your feet, and walk around any animal. It won't walk over your footprints. If you walk around a fire, then it will not burn beyond that boundary.

Approaching Birds[42]

If you can arrange it so that you get yourself a human skull and look through its eye sockets, then you can go as close as you want to birds.

To Prevent Someone from Leaving[43]

Take a sewing needle with which a corpse has been sewn into the shroud. Draw the needle through the hat, or the shoe of the one you wish to transfix. This cannot be undone.

To Overcome a Girl[44]

Take a coffin nail from a grave and some earth. Take it in all the names and put it into where a girl has pissed, while it is still warm, and say:

> *Teeth and tongue*
> *mouth and bone dust.*

"...all the names" being the Holy Trinity, or the saints & angels. This charm, for the rape of a girl, is shocking evidence of amorality and manipulation.

To Transfix a Bird in its Place[45]

First you look for the tree wherein the bird has its place to sing, or where it roosts during the night. When the bird has flown to its nest, take earth from the graves of three stillborn children, and a little ash from the oven, and mix together. Then you go around the place where you want the bird to be transfixed, and you should draw a four-rimmed circle, and on it spread a little of the earth, and say:

> *I [give both your, and your father's name]*
> *bind you to this place*
> *before 8 o'clock*
> *with words and earth*
> *with my 10 fingers*
> *and with 12 of God's angels.*

and then recite the Our Father in the four corners backwards four times; but whatever you do, don't look back when you leave there. This must be done in the names of:

> *God the Father*
> *and Son*
> *and Holy Ghost.*
> *Amen.*

Say this three times.

To Catch Fish[46]

I have been told that when you go fishing you should spread in the water a little earth that you have taken from the south church road together with fragments of rotten coffin. These ingredients should have been kept in a little purse. Then the fish will come forth.

To Make a Bird Stay in a Certain Place[47]

Take a corpse skull and write upon it the following:

> *Bide me*
> *bird on the branch*
> *as the dead man in the Grave*
> *in the name of the Father*
> *and of the Son*
> *and of the Holy Ghost.*

Take the skull in your right hand and walk around the place that the bird roosts and say:

> *Bide me*
> *bird*
> *in the name of the Trinity*
> *God the Father*
> *the Son*
> *and the Holy Ghost.*

Do this three times, then they cannot fly away from that place.

To Make a Bird Stay Still[48]

Take the foremost part of a skull. Then make three holes in it, one each Sunday during the sermon. Spy the bird through the hole and say:

> *Little bird on the next branch*
> *as the dead man in the grave*
> *in the name of the Father*
> *and of the Son*
> *and of the Holy Spirit.*

To Make a Seated Person Unable to Rise[49]

Whilst the priest stands over the grave during a funeral, you take a little earth from the grave. Take it with you outside the churchyard gate and swing yourself by the left heel widdershins three times and say:

> *In the name of the Holy Trinity.*

Then spread the earth on the head of someone who's sitting down, say:

> *Here you will sit as long as I wish*
> *in the name of God the Father*
> *and of the Son*
> *and of the Holy Ghost.*

To Make a Bird Stay Still[50]

Go to a cemetery on a Thursday evening, after the sun has set. Take a fragment of bone from near where the ear would have been. Write thereupon with your own blood and say three times:

> *I bind you Bird*
> *with my own blood*
> *and this in the name of the Father*
> *and of the Son*
> *and of the Holy Spirit.*
>
> *I bind you by heaven and earth*
> *by the sun and moon*
> *by the stars and planets*
> *and everything that God has created*
> *in heaven and on the earth*
> *and by all the holy martyrs and angels*
> *that you shall not escape from this circle.*

¶ Hexing with the Dead

*The bane of Death
is communicated to the victim by:*

*bone
coffin nail
graveyard earth
shroud needle
Troll-powder.*

Killing Someone[51]

In all secrecy, borrow a bone from a corpse and say:

> *Oh—you*
> *my brother, or sister, in the Christian faith*
> *loan me this bone.*

State your intent and establish the time period involved. Lay the bone unnoticed under the head of the one whose sleep you want to last for all eternity and say:

> *You**
> *will sleep*
> *and never wake up.*

Thereafter, the bone must be brought back to its resting place.

*Give the victim's name.

Hexing a Shotgun[52]

To magically destroy a shotgun, take a nail from a coffin and put it in the shotgun. As far as you put it down, then it is cursed, and no one can fix it thereafter.

To Hex a Shotgun[53]

Take a sewing needle that has sewn the corpse into a shroud, and stick it into the muzzle three times and pull on the lock and iron at once.

A Killing[54]

In Selanger, Sattna, Indal, Lidan, Holm and other parishes in Medelpad, there are various scary people, who practice their dark, devilish deeds yet to this very day. Although it is an era of enlightenment, I would say that Medelpad is no better today than it was under Karl the 9th's or Karl the 10th's reign—or in other words: it isn't any better now than five to seven hundred years ago, that time when witch-power was flourishing.

Have a look here at what is going on in the beginning of the twentieth century. Then, H. H. in Holm poached moose whenever he wanted. But then a farmer there thought that this was going too far, especially so since he discovered the poacher with a moose and reported the criminal. The result of this was that the poacher had to do six months at "The White Dove," as the Sundsvall Royal Prison is known. When he got out of there, he had thoughts of revenge towards the farmer who had informed upon him. He said:

> *Now I have served mine*
> *but you have yours left!*

He went to the churchyard and took a coffin nail, drew his enemy's image upon a fir tree and drove the nail into the chest of the figure. Some time afterwards the farmer began to pine away, and then it wasn't long before he died. When H. H. heard that, he said when drunk:

> *I thought that bastard would kick the bucket*
> *　in three years*
> *but that devil lived on for five.*

Another Account of the Same Killing[55]

There's a story about a magician-beggar, who had had a complaint lodged against him by a farmer for illegal moose-hunting. The magician hid in such a way, so that he could get to the graveyard one night and took a nail from a coffin. Then he went to the woods and painted the shape of the farmer on a fir tree, and then struck the nail into its chest, right over the heart. Afterwards he went to the farmer and said:

> *I have suffered my punishment*
> *now you have yours left.*

After that time, the farmer began to fade away. Each time the Wise One hit the nail a little further in, the farmer became ever weaker. He continued in this way for seven years, then he hit the nail into the figure's head, and then the farmer died.

To Give Someone Diarrhea[56]

Take a nail from out of a coffin. Nail it into his fæces.

To Hex a Shotgun[57]

Here's how: you take a common pin that has been passed over a corpse and put it into the barrel of the gun in both ends, and in the lock.

Or you only stick a finger into the mouth of a corpse, and then stick your finger into both ends of a shotgun barrel, and into the lock, then it is well and truly hexed.

To Send "Shot" at Someone[58]

It is a useful item if you can arrange to obtain a human skull at the beginning of the month of May. You plant peas during the summer, and keep it in a secure and secret hiding place. Come autumn, when the peas are fully ripe, pick them all yourself, so that they won't be used for anything else. When you want to shoot someone, then load your shotgun as usual with gunpowder but, for ammunition, take the peas instead of shot. But before you shoot them, you should draw the victim's picture, best likeness you can and then you say his and his father's name, and the three great Old Guys names. At the same moment have the shotgun in your hand and let it off without flinching. Then that person will receive that shot in the place on his body that you hit on the picture.

The motif of using a human skull and planting peas in the eye sockets is common. The usual reference to reciting the "Three Holy Names" is substituted with the less formal, some might even say irreligious "de 3 stora Gubbarnas namn," "In the name of the Three Big Guys." More than that, there is ambiguity as to which three guys are being referred to. Use of the names "Od Frö och Lok" (Odin, Freya, and Loki) persisted into the nineteenth century, and could be what is intended here.

Hexing a Fiddle[59]

A little graveyard earth strewn onto a fiddle, the strings will burn off.

So that a Tree or Bush will Wither Away[60]

Take a nail from a coffin that has been in a grave, and hit it into the root of the tree, then it will wither and die out.

Troll-Powder[61]

The poison is usually in bottles, mixed in with some liquid, but it also appears in pulverized form, and can then be given to the victim in coffee, alcohol, or baked with butter or cheese. The original and most feared corpse poison is procured from the skin of the body. My informant states that the corpse should have lain in the earth for approximately eight months. When buried for this long it begins to sweat, and the sweat then creates a shell of fungus on the exterior of the skin. This fungus is scraped off and bottled. Anyone who drinks of it will immediately become powerless. He will feel fierce burning in his stomach, and then the burning sensation moves up toward the chest, and the curse will then take root in the heart, the lungs, or the brain. As a rule, the poisoned one will become insane and then die soon afterwards.

A weaker type of troll-powder is procured from the earth with which the corpse has been in contact.

A third, less common, type of the poison is procured from the bones of the corpse which are ground up into a powder. The one who drinks of this type of poison shrivels up and in this way dies.

Punishing a Thief[62]

One could put a curse of diarrhea on someone by filling a hollow human bone with the excrement of a thief, and putting it in a swiftly moving stream.

To Triumph Over One Said to be Untouchable by Sword or Blows[63]

Whenever you have to face such a man, prepare yourself by finding a ring that is used in the marriage of three couples, this is put on the middle finger of the right hand. Then take a key that has been passed down for three generations, also a little lovage root. Then if you want to hit the hard man with a sword or saber, you should look for a man who died by the sword, or possibly a bullet. Collect the glazing off the body, and some clothes, and put it in the hilt and also take either three or nine hairs from his head and tie them around the saber-hilt. Then one can order one's saber to make as deep a wound as you want.

Beforehand, you can dig up a hole between two walls that are near to each other, and pass your saber through the hole, but whatever you do, do not let it touch the earth.

The only place where two walls are likely to be close enough for this to be practicable is where they meet at a corner, so a strange and special place is created to affect the sword. It is a void, but under the earth (which the sword must not touch) and is below two boundaries so, most likely, simultaneously both within and outside an enclosure. Having passed through this subterranean, neither-nor, liminal space the sword is ready to accept the influence of a man who died by violence. Thus armed, and fortified by symbols of family and property, one is ready to meet the challenge of a supernaturally protected foe.

To Cause Insanity[64]

Put graveyard earth into someone's coffee, little by little. They will go insane.

To Make a Horse Lame[65]

Take a nail from a rotten coffin, and three nails out of a horseshoe that has been found with the nails still in it. Smith it with the horseshoe nails. As you hammer them upon the anvil, say:

> *In the names of*
> *Belsebub*
> *Lucifer*
> *Belial*
> *and all the angels of Hell.*

The nail is struck without a head. It is made on a Thursday morning when the sun comes up. Push it into the hoof print of a horse and it will become lame. When it is removed, then the horse will be cured.

Observe: when the nail is taken, you should be silent, and when it is finished and being stored in the smithy.

This spell is reminiscent of one for stopping horses attributed to Guidon in a text first published as an appendix to the Grimoire of Pope Honorius in France in 1670. There, it is Beelzebub, Lucifer, and Satanas, who form the infernal triumvirate. A special nail is also forged during which, Guidon tells us, all Christian acts (such as prayers) must be eschewed. Here one has to stay silent, aside from naming of the angels of Hell.

To Make A Horse Lame[66]

Take three old horse-shoe nails, and a nail from a coffin that you have found in the churchyard. Hammer them in the middle of the hoof print, where the horse has walked. Then the horse will be lame, until the nails are removed.

The same procedure as the previous item, but without the infernal invocation.

To Make a Horse Lame[67]

If you're following after someone who is riding on a road, and you want to have his horse become lame, so that he won't outpace you, then take a nail and find the horse's footprint, where he has stepped on the road. Take the nail and pierce it, then the horse will become lame. The nail should be from a coffin.

This form of the spell is common in European folk magic.

To Drive Away Rats[68]

Malt is ground to flour, wherein is mixed finely ground human bone, taken from the churchyard. This is put out for the rats, so they flee away.

¶ The Dead Give Protection

*The living call upon the Dead
to guard them & their possessions.*

A Particular Bone[69]

The left ring finger of a corpse is good as a protective amulet. This finger of a dead man is a singularly good amulet of protection. If carried, no one can injure or shoot the bearer for a period of one day and one night. If a bullet is heading for the body, then it will rebound back and fall down harmlessly. It is the spirit of the bone who receives the bullet.

    The surest protective amulet is the left collar bone of the corpse of an aged man, as long as one buys it properly, and this should be done on a Thursday night during the waning moon.

So that No One Can Steal from Your Cart[70]

Take a sewing needle with a white silk thread and sew three times widdershins through the nose of a dead person, and then put the needle into the wagon before you load it.

Pray for Protection[71]

> *Go on to the graves*
> *fall upon your knees*
> *and pray to the dead.*

> *Receive protection*
> *so that they have peace.*

> *Those who do it.*

To Hinder Thievery and Fires[72]

Go to a graveyard when there are open graves and take a dead man's skull. Hide it in the cemetery. Go there in silence on a Sunday evening, then say:

> *I take you to use for my legitimate business*
> *during my lifetime.*

Then take the dead man's skull between your hands and say the following, as you circle your belongings. You may go as widely around them as you want:

> *You unnamed man*
> *I invoke you*
> *by the power of the name of the great triune God*
> *and Lord Jehovah*
> *and by the power of the names of Jesus Christ*
> *and of God the Holy Spirit.*

or only:

> *By the name of God the father*
> *of God the Son*
> *and of the Holy Spirit*

> *may you bind and transfix the hand of the thief*
> *on my goods*
> *until I return*
> *and keep fire away*
> *from my belongings*
> *and house*
> *and farm*
> *in the same power of the High Names*
> *who created me and you.*
> *Amen.*

N.B. This is said three times, as you walk three times around your belongings with the skull in your hands. Then put the skull on clean straw in a cupboard or trunk, under lock and key. This should all be done with proper respect.

Untried.

If You Want to Win When You Fight[73]

Carry a corpse tooth and a cockerel's egg in your clothes, then you can never be hit, even if you fight with someone.

A cock's egg is yokeless, and was traditionally thought to have been laid by a cockerel. Bestiaries stated such an egg, incubated by a toad or snake, hatched a cockatrice, which could petrify with its stare.

To Empower a Knife[74]

Sharpen, that is whet it, it on a gravestone. Say:

> *Whet out*
> *and whet in.*
> *The Power yours*
> *the Power mine*
> *and this will be united*
> *in the Mother of God*
> *Jesus Christ.*

Protecting a Shotgun[75]

To get your shotgun to be able to shoot far; and so that no one can hex it, then you should take some of the earth that the priest has thrown with his spade upon the coffin of a married woman who had identical twins. To that add:- the ash of a juniper tree; the heart of a bat; three snake-stingers: prepared quicksilver and three grains that have come whole and unharmed from the mill. Drill a hole under the point of the swan-screw, and put the powder down into the stock after it has been sewed into a piece of cloth from a cap of one who has been decapitated. Put some cloth from the right glove of the same man on the flint with a little of the juniper tree ash. Say the following three times:

> *In the name of God*
> *the Father*

and of the Son
and of the Holy Ghost.
Amen.

This charm requires two ingredients touched by miraculous fate. Identical twins are a biological wonder. The traditional horizontal mills of Scandinavia had cosmological significance. The moving upper stone symbolizing the heavens; the static lower stone—the earth and the watercourse beneath—the underworld. Grains that come unharmed through the mill are akin to a life on the surface of the earth that has escaped death. The heart of a bat and snake stingers (the forked tongue of snakes—widely believed to carry the venom) are considered hurtful, and therefore can provide protection from hurt. All are contained in cloth from a cap. Such headwear is not mentioned elsewhere in these texts. Usually, bones were the vehicle for the spirits of the Dead, but it seems that in the rare circumstance of decapitation, the spirit of the unfortunate man might rest in his hat.

When a Man has Been Hexed by an Evil Woman[76]

Take a corpse tooth and cense yourself with it, this will help.

If Your Shotgun is Hexed[77]

Take moss from a human skull. Put it between the gunpowder and the shot. Then fire the gun.

Moss from a human skull was an orthodox medicinal remedy that could be purchased from apothecaries in the seventeenth century.

If Your Shotgun is Hexed[78]

Dismantle the shotgun and then take some black crow chicks. Remove a kidney from one, as well as a little asafoetida and a little bit of graveyard earth. Use this mixture to polish the iron on the day when the Sun goes in Sp P J h. Thereafter no one will be able to hex the shotgun.

To Free Calves and the Cattle Shed from Bewitchment[79]

Having asked for it, take three handfuls of consecrated earth from the churchyard. Go around the cattle shed, preferably on Maundy Thursday morning. Throw one fistful of earth on the roof over the calf pens; then go three more times round the shed and throw the rest of the earth on three places on the roof. The cure is as good as done.

When a Horse has its Strength Stolen[80]

Take fragments from a decayed coffin, give it to the horse in its oats, but don't bring them under the roof.

¶ Winning with the Dead

*The Dead
invisible
beyond time
predict chance
and assist the gambler.*

To Win at the Lottery[81]

You go to the churchyard and borrow a human skull with these words:

> *I ask you my brother in Christendom*
> *or sister if you are*
> *that here rest in these bones*
> *in the name of the Holy Trinity*
> *in the name of God the Father*
> *and of the Son*
> *and of the Holy Ghost*
> *that I may borrow your head for three nights*
> *which I shall bring back at the same time*
>   *and place*
> *and I order you my brother or sister in*
>   *Christendom*
> *that upon the third night you come*
> *and tell me which numbers will come up in*
>   *the Royal Number Lottery.*

Then, take the skull and put it under the headpiece of your bed and the third night the dead one will come and will want his or her head back. Then you say to the corpse:

> *Tell me first the numbers that I order you*
> *then you shall have your head brought back.*

Then he will say all five numbers, and then you have to have a board on top of the blanket and a piece of chalk, and as quickly as the corpse says the numbers then write them down. But no light can be lit, and then the dead one will leave, and after that you must take back the head to its place again.

To Win at the Lottery[82]

Go on a Thursday evening to the churchyard and take a human skull and write on it the numbers you believe will come up. Return the next day, and retrieve the skull. The numbers that have been crossed out will not win, but the ones that have been left will come up, and those you will put into your hat, and then you'll win.

To Always Win at Gambling[83]

Take a needle with which a corpse has been sewn into a shroud, and stick it under the table where you're sitting and playing, then you can never lose. Or carry with you the herb that in German is called *Godsveis* in your right shoe. Or carry with you an owl's heart, then you won't lose, rather, you'll win.

To Win at Gambling[84]

Take a needle with which a corpse was sewn into a burial shroud, and stick into the underside of the table where you are sitting and playing cards, then you'll win.

¶ Shooting with the Dead

*The Dead
confer lethality
to gun and ammunition.*

The Correct Way to Shoot[85]

When autopsy is practiced upon a murderer, then his abdomen will be sewn back together. Take the needle with which this is accomplished and put it so that it will go into the butt-screw hole and then is screwed in. Then shoot with the shotgun at an animal, without taking care to aim, but you will surely hit your target even so.

The Correct Way to Shoot[86]

Take note when three hunters stand together on New Year's Day, then take moss from a dead man's skull, grind it and mix it with lead, then cast the bullet or shot from that, between 11 and 12 o'clock at night, without saying a word. When they've cooled, drop a little cotton-seed oil on them.

So that a Shotgun will Kill[87]

On a Thursday evening, after the sun has gone down, take some earth from the graveyard and pass it through the shotgun three times. Then, at the first opportunity, load the gun. When you have done this, carry the shotgun back and put the muzzle towards the floor and the stock upwards towards wood. Take the shotgun and shoot some kind of game bird and remove its heart. After you have recharged the gun with powder, load the heart and shoot it at this or that, then your shotgun will kill.

Here, the deathly quality of the graveyard earth is captured by loading it as quickly as possible, preserved by the gun being pointed towards the earth, and then distilled by shooting the heart of the first animal killed.

To Shoot and Hit Your Mark[88]

Take a corpse bone, dried, and grind it to powder, and mix it amongst the lead when you cast your shot, and some amongst the powder, and carry a little with you, then you'll always hit what you shoot at.

So that a Shotgun Will Kill[89]

Take a decayed bone at the churchyard, shave a little off with the nail, and then put it under the shot.

The Correct Way to Shoot[90]

Take a sewing needle with which a corpse has been sewn into its shroud, and break it apart into five pieces. Put four pieces of it underneath the butt, and the fifth with the eye where you usually hold your thumb, then one will hit the target that you're shooting at.

The Correct Way to Shoot[91]

The shotgun should be prepared in this way: take 2 measures of mercury, 2 measures of saltpeter, 4 measures of *adipis humanis* (human fat), and let it move inside the shotgun, and work it long enough that it comes up out of the muzzle. Or take a piece of wood from a coffin in which a mother who died in childbirth has lain, and insert a fragment into the butt of the shotgun, then whatever you shoot at will be hit.

It should be noted that, up until the eighteenth century, human fat was a recognized medical unguent available from apothecaries.

¶ Invisibility

*The spirits of the Dead are invisible
the Wise One may acquire this power.*

Through a Pea Grown in a Skull[92]

One goes to the churchyard on a Thursday night and borrows a bowl made from a skull's cranium, leaving a one-crown coin on the grave as payment. One places graveyard earth in the skull and puts it in a hollow tree or under a rocky outcrop, north of the church. Plant a pea in the earth. When the pea has grown and borne fruit, one takes a mirror and looks into it. One by one, put each pea in your mouth, until one comes to that pea that gives to you the power of invisibility. The very moment that pea goes into your mouth, your own image will disappear from the mirror. With that pea you can make yourself invisible whenever you please.

The sense of this ritual and the following ritual is that the dead person's spirit is drawn into the living plant as it sprouts forth from within the skull. The spirit then enters one of the peas, the one which gives the power of invisibility. Spells to achieve invisibility through peas grown in a skull are widespread in European folk magic, being recorded in a number of popular European printed grimoires.

Another with a Pea Grown in a Skull[93]

Take a human skull and bury it in the earth at a place that is wise, and put a pea through the eye in the skull, and let it grow and ripen. Then harvest them, open the pods, but be careful that you do not lose any of the peas. Then take one pea at a time, put it in your mouth and look in a mirror until you find the right one. Then you will not see your reflection in the mirror.

Invisible Like the Spirits of the Dead[94]

One buys a human bone on a Thursday night between twelve and one. Scrape it with a knife, so it becomes like flour. Take this flour and throw it over your head whilst saying:

> *With this I hide myself*
> *in the way of invisibility*
> *like the spirit that was*
> *at one time*
> *united with this bone*
> *and I leave my soul as security.*
> *Bornus Bister*
> *under the Devil's sigil*
> *in the name of God*
> *the Father*
> *and of the Son*
> *and of the Holy Ghost*

When one wants to once become visible again, thrust the knife into a tree, or into the wall of the house.

In this perilous working the Wise One leaves his soul as security "under the Devil's sigil" for the loan of the power of invisibility.

¶ The Spiritus

The Spiritus
a being in box or jar
perhaps given form
as scarab poppet
frog puppet
or found larva.

Here
a spirit of the Dead
is present with bone
and graveyard earth
or captured as a fly.

To Procure for Yourself Spirits[95]

Take unleavened bread that was baked on Sunday morning, or Saturday evening; either before or after the rising of the sun. Take just a crust and three new sewing needles made of thorn. Put the needles in a triangle in the bread and put three shillings worth of quicksilver into a prepared leather pouch that is sewn tight. Then late on Saturday evening, go to the churchyard and lay the pouch under a headstone of a man and say slowly:

> *Up and meet me.*
> *in the way that I shall order next Saturday*
>   *evening!*

The next Saturday evening, go there, touch the pouch and repeat:

> *Up and meet me.*
> *in the way that I shall order next Saturday*
>   *evening!*

On the third Saturday is said:

> *Up*
> *in the name of God*
> *the Father*
> *the Son*
> *and of the Holy Ghost*

> *and come to meet me here*
> *next Saturday night at midnight*
> *in the form of a fly upon my window*
> *then I shall take you into my service.*

Have a suitable little bottle to hand, cork it well and wrap it up and keep it with you so that you can catch the fly. When you want to know something, take the bottle in your hand, put it to your ear and speak slowly, then you will immediately get the right answer. But do not ask too much all at once, because then the fly will tire and suffer

N.B. Look out, that the bottle doesn't break, because then the spirit will get loose, and that will cost you your life.

When you die, if you keep the bottle that long, have it placed in your coffin so that it is buried with you, and then it will break. No other person may carry the bottle during your lifetime.

Untried

Obtaining One's Desires[96]

A person who was skilled in magic in Ransäter had a so-called "Spiritus" [Swedish: *spertus*]. The being was held in a round brass box which was filled with graveyard earth and "a dead man's bone." When it had been filled the lock was turned so that it could not be opened. On the lock there was a knob with a notch, like the sights of a rifle.

When the Spertus was to be used, its owner went to the crossroads during the new moon and stood at the very middle of the two roads and looked at the very tip of the new moon through the sighting notch on the box, and at that very moment wished for something. Then that wish would be fulfilled.

A woman who knew magic in Nyed parish also had a Spiritus. It was also a brass box in which she had placed the larva of a type of butterfly together with green leaves and over time it happened that she wished things of it. This Spiritus had especially the ability to draw money to its owner.

There were several kinds of Spiritus, but all had this one thing in common, that they would finally destroy their owners. The Spertus was actually the Devil himself, and for payment for the good done to the owner, he took them in the end.

It is to be noted that it is an inbetween or liminal state that is sought for this working, you stand at a point from whence four roads lead just as the dark moon turns to light, then, at that time and place, the spiritus may carry out the will of the Wise One.

¶ The Rune-Stone

*The red Rune-Stone
exchanged by the Dead
for a pact with Beelzebub
written in blood.*

*It summons the Dead
and gives many powers.*

The Runestone[97]

To conjure forth invisible spirits so as to be able to speak to them in order to find out hidden things.

    First, using your own blood, write these letters and your name upon an old chip of evergreen wood.

*Filler # ℈ aKteol hórdaa
℞ ⅐ 2 2 Pilack Bjälfebub
behöfver*

On a Thursday evening go to the churchyard and put the chip of wood under an earth-fast stone. As you do so, say your name and ask the spirits to meet you on the following Thursday evening. When you go there for the second Thursday evening, take the shaving and state their name as well as saying the following:

> *I command you N.N.*
> *that you come to meet me*
> *on the next coming Thursday evening*
> *this in the name of*
> *God the Father*
> *The Son*
> *And the Holy Ghost*

Then go there on the third Thursday evening. You will find the shaving has gone and a little runestone is there instead. Take this stone and keep it. Then, they will come to you. You can ask them anything you wish to know, but don't ask them too much the first time, otherwise they will become unhappy. But thereafter, you may know of the nature of the book.

1. When you have this runestone in your purse, then you will never be short of money.

2. When you put the stone in a glass bottle and shake it, then the spirits will come to you, wherever you are. If you don't want to have more than one, then just shake the bottle once. But if you want to have several, then you should shake the bottle once for each one that you wish to appear. For as soon as you have that stone, then they are bound to serve you and do everything that you order them.

3. They will tell you everything that you wish to know in the whole wide world.

4. If you want to fight and have this stone in your clothes, then you will never get beaten.

5. If you have the stone in your purse and hang the purse under your left arm and then go out and gamble, then you will win as often as you wish.

6. If you desire it so that no court will punish you, before you go to court, place the runestone in your left shoe. Then no judge can condemn you, nor any witness testify against you.

7. If you have the stone in your mouth and wish for something from someone, whether it is little or big, they will be enchanted and will not be able to deny you what you wish.

8. If you are in dispute with someone, then put the stone under your tongue, then you cannot be out talked by any person.

9. If you have the stone on you and want a maiden to love you, then take her in your embrace, and then she will love you obsessively.

10. If you want to shoot, take the stone and put it into the shotgun case, then the animals will come forward to you, and you can shoot them as quickly as you have time to load.

11. If you wish to win the lottery, take the money out of the purse and put the stone in it. Leave it there for three days and three nights. Then take the same money and put it into the lottery, then you'll win.

12. If you take the stone and put it on your head, then you are invisible for all people.

13. As long as you have that stone, then you will have luck in everything that you will begin, whatever it may be.

14. If you put the stone under your left foot and want to walk on water, then you will be able to go dry-shoed. If you put the stone at your knee and then go on water, then you will go down into the water to your knees, and however far up you put the stone on your body, that's as far as you will sink in the water.

15. Even if you are far away, but you want to get home in an hour, then you take three drops of blood and anoint the stone and say:

I wish that I were home.

A spirit will appear and carry you home, but you won't know how you got there.

16. This stone is red of colour, and no larger than a nut. Once you have had it for a year, then it will not leave you. If you throw it into a lake or fire, it will come back to you again. But, after you have had it for fifty years, then don't keep it any longer. Then you can be rid of it by selling it to someone else or take it back to the place you got it from, and then you can get rid of it there.

The meaning of the blood drawn *trollkaraktärer* [troll letters] is elusive, the last two words of the inscription translate as "Beelzebub needs."

¶ The Ring-Belt

*Lycanthropy
arcturanthropy
transformations achieved
by passing through the deathly Ring-Belt.*

The Ring-Belt[98]

The practice of clothing oneself in a form of an animal is a tradition which our forefathers amongst both the Sámi and the Swedes knew well, however very few are able to succeed in this endeavour and, those that do often lose their mind.

To acquire the ability to take on the shape of an animal, whether it be that of a bear or a wolf, one must first procure a belt that has magical power. This belt, which is made of human skin, is obtained on a Thursday night – preferably towards Christmas, Pentecost, or some other of the greater holidays between twelve and one, from a corpse that one digs up in the graveyard. Preferably, it should be a man's corpse. The belt is taken from around the corpse's waist and is about three or four thumbs wide. One uses a knife to flay it off, taking care that it is undamaged in the process. One who owns such a belt can, whenever he wishes, take the shape of a bear or a wolf. To transform yourself, do the following: creep, headfirst, through the belt three times. The first time one creeps through it one gets the head of the animal, the second one is half animal, and the third time the transformation is complete. When one wants to return to human shape again, one creeps with the feet first through the belt, three times as before.

It was about thirty-five years ago, when in my travels I came to a village in Ramsele, Västra Vimmelvattnet, where they told me about a man who had such a belt. A few years before my arrival, they hired the Sámi Anders Fjällmark as a horse grazer, whose job it was to take care of the animals for several villages. When the autumn came and Fjällmark brought the horses back to receive his remuneration, there was a mean, rich farmer, who didn't want to pay the fee. Fjällmark became very angry over this, and said that since the farmer didn't want to pay willingly, then both wolf and bear would devastate his cattle and horses. The farmer only laughed at his threats and said that if the Sámi didn't leave off, he would throw him out. The Sámi left.

But when he came to the woods, he took his belt-ring and transformed himself into a bear, went and mauled the farmer's horses, so that he lost the animals. Then, he took a wolf shape and savaged all the cows, sheep, goats, and hens, so that the farmer had no livestock left. Finally, Fjällmark set loose lice and vermin on the greedy farmer, and he suffered from these parasites for the rest of his life.

Another time, this same Fjällmark was in Jämtland, in Hammardals parish, where he lived one summer with his family. On one occasion he was in the woods and was helping some farmers bringing in the firewood. One night, the seasonal workers were sleeping in a hay barn. One of the girls awoke when Fjällmark went out. As she was lying close to the barn wall she could peek out through the cracks, so she could see what it was that Fjällmark was doing outside. She saw how he took forth something out of the folds of his sweater and crept through – it was the remarkable ring-belt. Then she saw how Fjällmark was, step by step, transformed into a bear. The girl, naturally, was petrified with fear and could neither move nor call out to anyone. In a while, the bear returned and took again its human shape.

When day came, she described for the farmer what she had seen. He could not believe what he had been told, but asked her not to reveal to anyone else what she had seen. The farmer began to spy on Fjällmark and when he had fallen asleep one time; he managed to steal the ring-belt from him. Then, when he had it in his hands, he threw it in the fire to destroy it. But, as it became surrounded by flames, it hurled itself back. The second time he threw it on the fire, it was thrown back as before. But the third time it stayed there and was burned to ashes. During that time, Fjällmark agonized greatly in his sleep, broke out in a cold sweat, and threw himself back and forth. But after that time, Fjällmark lost his ability to transform himself into a wolf or a bear.

There is another method to procure for yourself such a ring-belt which I heard from an old Sámi called Paulus August Nilsson of Nora Parish. He learnt it from his parents. To obtain such a belt, do the following. Between twelve and one at night, on a Thursday or a feast day, go to place where a suicide or another corpse has been buried. Take from the corpse the sinew that runs down the left arm to the hand. From such sinew spin threads and make rope in the form of a ring large enough so that one can creep through it. Do this, and you have the ability to transform yourself into a bear or wolf.

A magic belt by which a man transforms into a werewolf is an important feature of German folklore. This narrative describes how it was used to supernaturally attack horses and other livestock. Guidon, *Magical Secrets* (Society of Esoteric Endeavour) infers in obscene terms that seventeenth-century blacksmiths in Normandy might take the form of wolves to injure the horses of rivals. In Britain, mysterious mutilations of horses continue into the present day, though supernatural explanations for such attacks are now forgotten.

¶ Some Warnings

Returning the Bones[99]

No matter what, before their own death, the Wise One must put back what he took from the Dead. Otherwise, he would have no peace in the grave. There was a man who emigrated to America who was, according to accounts, finally forced to make the long journey home, to put back what he had borrowed from the churchyard.

Protective Amulet[100]

A good protective amulet is obtained if one takes a one-crown piece and bores a hole in it and threads a black silk thread through the hole. Then one takes hold of the thread, without touching the coin, and lays the coin in the mouth of a suicide. This is a good amulet, which can be used to reveal thieves and evil people and to attract money or other things, whatever one desires. When one puts the coin in the mouth of the suicide, then one can wish three wishes. If one puts the coin in alcohol, then one can see thieves and other people in the liquor.

But when, one day, you leave the earthly plane, then you will have regrets. I have seen such a person's journey into death and if I lived to the age of Methuselah, I'd never be able to forget it. It was the most frightening thing that I have seen in all my life. Foam came from his mouth, and he screamed as he suffered terribly. He could hear and see the sufferings of the damned.

Afterword
The Wise & Their World

AS late as 1958, Swedish folklorist Carl-Herman Tillhagen made a case for the continuity of the practice of *klokskap* (lit. *wisdom*), or use of folk magic, from as early as the Bronze Age in the first millennium BCE, all the way to the more modern practice of folk healing and sorcery in Sweden.[101] Tillhagen followed a distinguished line of Swedish folklorists who pursued this same line of reasoning: J. J. Törner (1787), L. F. Rääf (1843), C. W. von Sydow (1878-1952), G. Ericksson (1878). E. Linderholm (1927-39), and C-M Bergstrand (1932). All understood the continuity of folk magic and medicine with what had preceded it, in a past whether pagan or priestly.

What we know of the earliest magical practices is generalized primarily from archaeological evidence. With the passage of time, oral traditions and written sagas preserved what was left of a well-rounded practice of folk magic. These traditions did not end with bronze-age archaeology or medieval literature, however. In Sweden, and Scandinavia generally, we have always had the Wise Ones, *de kloka*, who worked healing and hexing, divination and transfixing, and exercised their considerable control over folk and livestock well into the twentieth century. In my research at the Nordic Museum in Stockholm (Sw. *Nordiska muséet*) in the early 1990s, the most recent collection of spells and magic to which I had access was a manuscript that was still being written in 1941 by Elsa Halmdahl, a practitioner of these arts in Stockholm.[102]

The wise were always predisposed to seeing the world differently. Their perceptions included what most might dismiss as signs of mental instability. These were, for example, being able to see and speak with spirits of the dead, calling up winds, altering hunting luck by means of various manipulations of the hunting rifle or fish net, or conjuring the spirit of the prey. They included creating illusions to frighten, and concocting medicinal tinctures and plasters to administer to the ill and suffering. Conjuring forth the image of a thief in a tumbler of whiskey by first blessing it with one's sorcerer's knife (Sw. *trollgubbekniv*) was a skill that was much in demand in a rural life that did not know sophisticated locks. Even better was when the stolen goods were returned, with the thief left maimed in some way as a warning to others who might be overly trusting.

The wise were clever at manipulating public opinion as well. One tale tells of Anders i Alehagen being warned that he was under magical attack by a wise woman in a neighboring parish. Boasting, he belittled the magical skill of his alleged adversary, saying "Oh, she only has eleven, but I have twelve."[103] The folklore collector makes a parenthetical comment that this was meant to refer to serving or familiar spirits, in Swedish called *spertusar*. Another collection mentions Mor Lisa i Finshult (Lisa Katrina Svensdotter), who had an eye ailment that resulted in the shrinking of her eyeballs. When she wished to impress upon someone her status as a powerful healer, she would insert tufts of wool or yarn into the sockets to frighten them.[104]

To be sure, Sweden was not the only country to see a continuation of folk magic and healing through millennia. It was a cultural phenomenon that existed all over the European continent and beyond, and in Sweden was a local manifestation or reflex of what could be called a pan-European Folk Magic Culture. In its own way, it also represented a unique cultural confluence of currents from at least three areas: a circumpolar shamanic culture represented by the Sámi lore collected in the North, a native healing tradition that had its own, more native herbal *materia medica*, and a shared European body of lore that came up through Germany and Denmark, and which included lore from the Middle East and Northern Africa. This last was the subject of much academic work in the 1950s by scholars such as Will-Erich Peukert (1954) and Carl-Martin Edsman (1946, 1959, 1962). In these studies, textual relationships between the Swedish Black Art Books and the continental grimoires, which were called in Danish *Cyprianer* and which Peukert calls in German *Hausväterlitteratur*, were explored. Recent work by Professor Owen Davies at the University of Hertfordshire shows that the English reflex of this pan-European folk magic culture bears many similarities to its neighbors', both in practice and in the presence of the phenomenon of the Black Art Book (Davies, 2003, 2009).

As with any confluence of currents, one must be wary of over-generalizing. The diversity of sources requires care in analysis, and doctrinal statements about such a pluralistic tradition are made in vain. To the extent that traits are shared, however, one can joyfully recognize similarities in trends, approaches, views, and practices.

For example, one factor that is important in all folk magic is its traditional quality—it is handed down, and typically shows some conservatism in that transmission. Things which are not repeated are not traditional. Sometimes, words are the conserved trait, with ritual actions open to spontaneous improvisation. At other times, the ritual action is the conservative element, and the spoken or chanted charm which accompanies it is created anew for each performance. Along this same line of reasoning, the age of a spell, or a spell book, is important to bolster a belief in its efficacy. If a procedure or spell had not been effective, it would not have survived through the centuries to be recorded in the present.

Another trait of folk magic is its reliance on power objects. These are sometimes objects found in nature that display some unusual quality or appearance. Sometimes, however, they are items created by the craftsman, and derive their power by ritual performed over them, such as the small magical boxes (Sw. *trollaskar*) which contain carved pieces of wood or worked stone, and which were considered an adjunct in the wise one's spellcrafting. A related idea to power objects is the idea of power plants.

The *materia medica* of folk medicine that the wise ones practiced contained not just plants, however. We have substances that recall Renaissance theurgy and alchemy, such as sulfur and liquid mercury. Animal parts such as castoreum (Sw. *bäfvergäll*, essentially beaver musk) were common ingredients in plasters as well as potions. Gun powder was also prescribed to be taken internally. Perhaps gun powder was popular because of its volatility, and thus its power to induce activity and health in the patient. Some of these power substances are shared across Europe, and some even with East Asian Medicine.

The magic of place was also important in the Wise Ones' craft. Trees with unusual shapes, or that had branches that had grown in such a way that they fused together to form a gap (Sw. *smöjträ*) through which items or people might be passed, were important in bringing about magical results. Folk healing was often performed with such a *smöjträ*, or wooden ring. Sometimes the patient's name would be changed after this performance, so that the passage through the ring emulated a type of rebirth, one without the prior affliction. With a different name, the infective agent would find it difficult to find its prior victim.

Places where roads meet, sometimes crossroads, but often places where three roads meet, contained a magical charge. Often, the practitioner would bury an object or offering in its vicinity so that it would absorb this charge.

In the Swedish tradition, movements were prescribed to happen in particular directions, and toward various quarters. For example, Tillhagen[105] writes that any circular movement should always occur "against the sun" (Sw. *ansyls*, *avig*), and if something is to be thrown, it should be over the left shoulder. The directions of power were the North and the West—a northward running stream or the north side of a tree are both places of power and afford powerful aid. The repetition of a formula three times, the proscription not to look back after obtaining a magical object, or leaving an offering, the admonition to remain silent about the working, and the prohibition against thanking the healer after a working: all of these were at work in the tradition. Even nakedness had its place in both healing and in working magic.

And of course, the realm of the Dead, the cemetery or churchyard, participated especially in the magic of place. As the selection of spells and charms in this collection shows, the place (often an enclosed space around parish churches), its contents (bones, skulls, and graveyard dirt), and the contacts it might hold with spirits of the dead were all reasons the churchyard was important in the practice of folk magic. Just as the vehicle of magical change was hidden, with cause and effect often invisible to observer and practitioner alike, so were the spirits of the dead from whom one sought favors. But the physical artifacts, the dirt and the bones, were immediate reminders of this hidden company of souls with whom the wise worked.

That we know anything at all about the Wise in Sweden is the result of folklore gathering efforts there, especially between the seventeenth and twentieth centuries. During this time, the Swedish government made it a priority to gather what was known about folklore and customs throughout the realm. As a result, folklore became "folk treasure" (Sw. *folkskatt*), and individuals educated in interview techniques were sent out from universities and governmental bodies to gather this treasure and bring it back to catalogue and preserve. Included in this gathering effort were folk narratives, oral magical charms, healing and ritual procedures, and hand-written manuscripts of folk spells called "*svartkonstböcker*" or black art books. Sometimes entire manuscripts were surrendered to these collectors, but more often, the collectors were allowed to copy whatever they might in an effort to present a well-rounded picture of the general practice of folk healing and magic in its time and place. In this way, they were always dated, and as much information about practitioner and locale was gathered as possible. Swedish folklore archives are unusual in the fact that they seek to capture as much contextual information as possible. With all this information, we can surmise quite a good deal about who these Wise Folk were, where they lived, and how they practiced their art. We have names, birth and death dates, locations, church records, stories about their practice, and about other wise folk in their vicinity.

For example, we have a large range of terms that were used for these magical practitioners, each with their own story. *Smältgumman*, or "melting woman," was one name, because one technique used by the Wise Ones was to melt either wax or lead and pour it into a pail of cold water, and from the shapes of the solidified substances they could divine the cause of illness or give body to the alien spirit's shape. If molten lead was used to give it shape, then the Wise One may have had the name "*blygumman*" or "lead-woman." Another commonly used term was "*kukkelgubbe*" or "*kukkelgumma*"—sorcerer or sorceress, from an Old Norse term meaning to work magic. *Lövjerska* (fem.) or *lövjare* (masc.) come from the Old Norse "*lyf*" meaning "healing or poisoning substances." "*Kusla*" and "*kusme*" come from a common root meaning to do magic by means of incantation, hence "*kusmegubbe*" or "*kuslakärring*." Often, wise folk would take their names from either the place they worked, or the type of work they did: *Ben*-Lasse (bone-healing Lars), or Anders *i Alehagen* (Anders from Mandrake Meadow). And finally, the Wise Ones were also called "church yard wanderers" (Sw. *kyrkogårdsgångare*) because much of the power they derived was from an interaction with the Dead, and their Realm. The Swedish *kyrkogård* can be translated as either "churchyard" or "cemetery." Many Wise Ones obtained the powers they wielded from power objects obtained from the cemetery, or through the intercession of dead spirits.

There is no doubt that at least part of the function of the Wise Ones in Sweden was to serve as medical providers in a rural society that had misgivings about a newly rising and costly medical profession. But there is also a subtlety here. Health can be understood in larger terms than the strictly physical or medical. It was as likely that the causes of disease were to be found in something as mundane as tooth decay as it was to be found in the "overlooking" of a jealous neighbour. Misfortune from being burgled was as likely to be from a condition of ill health as it was of ill luck. In such a world, those who healed and those who hexed were interpreters of natural phenomena. They sought the cause, and its correction for the people. This has sometimes resulted in the overgeneralization that the Wise Ones were only folk-medical healers. Greater attention needs to be paid by specialists to categories of both folk illness and ill luck, of both medicine and magic.

Theoretically speaking, ill health in folk and livestock was often credited to "worms" (Sw. *torsk, orm*) that had invaded the flesh of the patient. This is an idea with roots back to a pan-European folk medical understanding, which includes the Anglo-Saxon charm corpus and the Merseburg charms. If not worms, then the most likely culprit was elf-shot (Sw. *trollskott*), either from a jealous neighbor or from an offended nature spirit such as the wood- or water-sprite (Sw. *skogsrå*; *sjörå*). All required that materials be gathered, whether for incense or herbal soak, for plaster or for potion. In almost all cases, divination was the method of diagnosis. One common method of diagnosis was to take a head scarf, and fold it in four horizontal folds with one's knife at the first innermost fold. One then took it and swept it nine times around the patient's head. If the blade of the knife became exposed from the folds of the scarf during the procedure, the diagnosis of the illness was established.

The Wise Ones lived on the edges of social acceptability. They participated as much in village life as they did in the open desolate places haunted by forest sprite and nixie. They knew the church or ecclesiastical year as well as an older pagan pantheon that allowed them to call upon either demons of the infernal hierarchy such as Beelzebub, or non-Christian nature spirits such as the farm wight (Sw. *tomtegubbe*) to imbue their spells with power. Because the Wise Ones participated, at least initially, in homogeneous Swedish society, some were able to receive a state-sponsored education. They were taught to read and write.

The material you have in this volume is the result of reading and writing (i.e., literate) Wise Ones from Sweden whose lives spanned a period from the late 1600s to the mid 1900s. They were each inheritors of lore from periods before this, as is shown by remnants of Roman Catholic ritual which remain in the texts. The conversion to Protestantism occurred in Sweden officially in 1523, long before these texts were written down. We know however that the version of Christianity that was in place was not well established, with many families persisting in folk customs that much more resembled those of their pagan ancestors. Saint Birgitta of Vadstena wrote in her *Revelations* (Sw. *Uppenbarelser 6:28*) over three and a half centuries after the official conversion to Roman Christianity that it was still common among the folk of the area to make offerings of cattle, swine, bread, wine, and other drinks to the "tomte god" (Old Sw. *tompte gudh*). Offerings are unapologetically still being made today to the *tomte* or farm wight, both in Scandinavia and among expatriates.

Writing styles in manuscripts originating in southern Swedish provinces often show continental influence, such as in the use of the German *Fraktur* (so-called Gothic) handwriting style. These southern grimoires typically use herbal names that are either calques (literal translations) or direct loans of names of continentally growing herbs. Locally growing herbs mentioned in recipes from central and northern provinces suggest grimoires that were more likely created within Sweden using native healing lore.

The books were themselves enshrouded with lore. They were supposed to be written in ink composed in some cases of blood. In others, the pages were black, with letters of white.[106] Concern for discovery and persecution were clearly evident in some, as whole sections were enciphered, using a numerical substitution for alphabetical representation. Power substances, references to heretical use of church property, the sacraments, or to demonic spirits were written in this cipher. Whether this was to avoid discovery, or to preserve the secrets of the art from prying eyes is a matter for conjecture.

Some spells included what have in Swedish been called Wittenberg Letters (Sw. *Wittenbergska bokstäver*) or magical-characters (Sw. *trollkaraktärer*) They were figures sometimes based on letters of the alphabet, but more often were sigils of some type that lent power to the spell. In this, they functioned much like the sigils found in the *Lemegeton* or *Goëtia*. They were often meant to be drawn on either virgin paper or parchment (i.e., paper or parchment that had not previously had writing on it), and carried on one's person. At some times, they were drawn as a part of a longer spell, and inserted into the keyhole of the church, or left under its threshold. At others they were folded and kept in one's shoe, or otherwise close to the skin. These magical letters evoked the power that was used to accomplish the aim of the accompanying text.

Perhaps most importantly, the book itself was a magical fetish, a power object, the mere possession of which guaranteed magical power, regardless of any ability to read it. One tale tells of an unwitting assistant opening a volume and releasing a host of demonic spirits, which required their eventual recapture by the book's true owner. Another tale tells of how the ever-increasing weight of the volume prevented an assistant from fetching the book for their master. This required the master's eventual intervention. Perhaps this was a metaphor for the weight of learning it contained, or perhaps the slippery nature of the Black Art?

These compendia of lore were carefully guarded, and narratives suggest that when such a black art book was passed on to another, the sorcerer could well lose the power it bestowed. The lore it contained was not sufficient for a complete understanding of the practices of magic, but it was clear that with such a book in one's possession, one had the power to hex or heal, to bind or to loose, to give luck or to take it away, to hush the mouths of false witnesses, to transfix prey, thieves, or enemies, and to hear even the speech of birds. These books of the Black Art (Sw. *svartkonstböcker*) were more than mere textbooks. They were allies in the practice of the Dark Art. And they continue to exist, and whisper their secrets to us through dark corridors of infernal scriptoria even today.

Tom Johnson, PhD
16 July 2012

REFERENCES

1 C-H Tillhagen, *Folklig Läkekonst* (Stockholm: Nordiska Muséet, 1958), 78.
2 IFGH448, s.1-3, Lars Johan Samuelsson. uppt. Elin Emannelsson, 1928 Öxabäck, Västergötland.
3 Tillhagen, *Folklig Läkekonst*, 78 collected in Skredsvik parish, Bohuslän.
4 Nordiska muséet MS Nº 271.601 Läkarbokf [The Book of Healing] Elsa Halmdahl, Stockholm, 1929, item Nº 103. Thomas K. Johnson, *Svartkonstböcker: A Compendium of the Swedish Black Art Book Tradition* (Seattle: Revelore Press, 2019), 452. Much of the ms is her record of instructions received from her teacher Olle Åberg of Gåltjärn (d. Sept 10, 1932). Some were acquired after his death, by means of visions and dreams. The inside of the front and back covers records the names of well over sixty Wise Ones known to Halmdahl.
5 Nordiska muséet MS Nº 271.601 Sankt Petri Nyckel [The Key of Saint Peter], item Nº 36 in ms also compiled by Halmdahl 1939-40. Johnson, *Svartkonstböcker*, 430. She carefully records her source for each item, the charm's power being seemingly related to its provenance. This item she acquired from "P.S." The British references to such flutes can be found in Nigel Pennick, *Secrets of East*

Anglian Magic, Hale 1995 and Andrew Chumbley, *One, the Grimoire of the Golden Toad*, Xoanon, 2000.

6 LUF, MSS A, B, C, Signerier och Besvärjelser [Spells and Conjourations], Jon Johansson Svartkonstbok [Black Arts Book] from Mo, Rådom, Västnorrlands län, Lappland, item No.9 which was acquired from J. A. Åberg of Karlsmyran. Johnson, *Svartkonstböcker*, 338. When Johansson sent this record of his and other Sámi Wise Ones practice to folklorist C. W. von Sydow in Lund, he wrote:

By sending these to you. I have surrendered my power, that is to say I no longer have the power to stop bleeding and such. It isn't "humbug" as modern folk say about so called "kukkelgubbar"[magicians] because such wisdom in words and spells finds its origins all the way back to Christ's time when the Saviour walked here on Earth and because he gave his disciples power to heal all sorts of sicknesses, make the blind see, resurrect the dead, etc. Because we are also his disciples, because we believe, but we cannot work wonders for those who don't believe, and unfortunately, there aren't many believers...

7 Tillhagen, *Folklig Läkekonst*, 129.
8 Johansson, Spells and Conjurations, item N⁰ 8, a ritual he learned from J. A. Åberg, Karlsmyran. Johnson, *Svartkonstböcker*, 338.
9 MS KUIII20 Svartkonstbok [Black Arts Book] Slimminge socken, Vemmenhögs härad, Skåne, 1853. item N⁰ 121. Johnson, *Svartkonstböcker*, 293.

It would appear that this ms was compiled by a blacksmith as it contains numerous mundane metallurgical recipes and instructions.

10 Nordiska muséet MS № 271.602 Negromänliska saker [Necromantic/Nigromantic Matters—the MS title may mean either], item № 2 much of this ms is copied from a seventeenth-century German printed book attributed to Faust. Johnson, *Svartkonstböcker*, 465.

11 MS Supriania Fru Alstads Socken, Skytts härad, 1858, item № 5. Johnson, *Svartkonstböcker*, "To conjure up a dead person," 430. The ms has 17 items mostly devoted to healing. The title is a variant spelling of Cyprianus, considered to be the patron saint of sorcerers. A number of different magical texts are attributed to him.

12 MS ULMA 36365, Salomoniska magiska konster [Solomon's Magical Arts] Nöttebäck-Granhult parish, Småland. Johnson, *Svartkonstböcker*, 573. This ritual is item № 70 in the ms, which dates from the middle of the eighteenth century. It carries this remarkable illustration on the first page:

13 Halmdahl, Book of Healing, item Nº 88 being acquired from Adolf Lundkvist, a Sami in September 1936. Johnson, *Svartkonstböcker*, 452.
14 Tillhagen, *Folklig Läkekonst*. Collected from Korsberga in Västergötland.
15 Tillhagen, *Folklig Läkekonst*. Collected from Ekesbog in Västergötland.
16 EM 3329 B ["Nº 4 Stora katekis [Nº 4 The Great Catechism,] Bengt Ahlström, Eslöv, 1865, item Nº 36. Johnson, *Svartkonstböcker*, 255. This MS records the teachings of Ahlström who died in 1919, aged 92. A talented carpenter, he turned from woodwork to healing, becoming known as "The Professor." He was described as a pleasant and talkative man with quite an extensive library. An elderly native of Eslöv said of him:

The poor always went to professor Ahlström. The real doctors were too expensive for anyone to be able to afford going to them. Professor was a talented man who could cure all sorts of sickness. You could have a pain wherever, and he could get rid of the evil. He was inexpensive and knowledgeable... There were always terribly many people at his place. He didn't just heal people, but animals as well, for example pigs that had bone sickness. The farmers often came with a heifer or a horse for him...

17 Johansson, Spells and Conjurations, item No.6 in the supplement to ms B. Johnson, *Svartkonstböcker*, 346.

18 Ahlström, Rademin, item Nº 37. Johnson, *Svartkonstböcker*, 243: "Your pain shall disappear as a dead person that is in the earth lies in the name of the F and S and the H Gh, three times."
19 Ahlström. Nº 4 The Great Catechism, item Nº 8. Johnson, *Svartkonstböcker*, 248.
20 Halmdahl, The Book of Healing, item Nº 58. She received this ritual from a Wise One named Vallin. Johnson, *Svartkonstböcker*, "Vallins recitation to be able to See," 447–48: "In the names of all 7 of the spirits of the abyss, I command you to appear and tell me what this man or woman has for sicknesses. You spirits of the abyss tell me, and bow down before the most powerful God the Son the Holy Ghost and in the name of the Virgin Mary. Cross me 9 times, first head, then chest. To [kusma] this, go to a grave, take up a plant with the roots. Recite this while you take it. Keep it inside afterwards. Recite this: when I take you, the one who lies in this grave, does not deny me this root that I take for many blessings. Rather give me your power and blessing. Rest heavily in your gave. I wish you no ill. Work peacefully in God's name. Vallin."
21 Johansson, Spells and Conjurations, item Nº 3 in the supplement to ms B. Johnson, *Svartkonstböcker*, "Bad Ache and *Ränsel*," 345–46.
22 Nordiska muséet MS Nº 33.824, item Nº 18. Johnson, *Svartkonstböcker*, 360. This ms has inscriptions which list some owners, the first being Erik Länmark in Spånga, with the date

1838. Then comes Carl Lager from Länna Works and then Amanda Josefina from Åkers parish in Södermanland where the MS was discovered in 1886. Occasionally code is used; in this charm all mention of the use of human bones is enciphered.

23 Solomon's Magical Arts, item Nº 125. Johnson, *Svartkonstböcker*, 586.
24 Nordiska muséet MS Nº 33.824 item Nº 1. Johnson, *Svartkonstböcker*, 357: "*Flen* is a dialect word that, according to Rietz, means different things in various localities. In southern Sweden, it has to do with an upset stomach, pain or discomfort from acid indigestion, &c. In northern Sweden, it has more to do with a reddened and painful swelling of the skin." Johnson, *Svartkonstböcker*, 357 Nº 86. A body in the woods sounds like that of a murder victim.
25 Nordiska muséet ms Onumrerad [Unnumbered] Åkers härad, Södermanland item Nº 30. Johnson, *Svartkonstböcker*, 521.
26 MS KU 3335, Trollboken, [Magic Book], Erik Johan Arborén. Lakbäck, Rogsta socken, Hälsingland, private ownership, item Nº 26. Johnson, *Svartkonstböcker*, 272. Arborén worked as a fisherman, farmer, and businessman in Lakbäck. He compiled this MS when aged 17. Pusten, a Wise One, was a squatter in Västanbäck, Rogsta parish. He was away for the day and Arborén managed to persuade his wife to lend him her husband's Black Book. He copied as much as he could, creating

this manuscript, before he had to rush to get the book back before Pusten returned. Enigmatically, the ms commences with this inscription: "My oath is broken. This Ekonomia or Maria Christina Naturalia Belongs to Erik Johan Andersson Rogsta Västanbäckk The 15th of August, 1881." It is not clear what oath has been broken. There are also some subsequent ownership inscriptions, namely: Gustav Åström 1819 and 1823, and Jonas Magnus Åström 1850.

27 Ahlström, N⁰ 4 The Great Catechism, item N⁰ 51 *op cit.* Johnson, *Svartkonstböcker*, 258. *Stroke* may be either the same as in English, or the stroke of a færy whip causing a painful raised swelling.

28 Tillhagen, *Folklig Läkekonst*. Recorded in Nödinge in the Västergötland Södermanland area.

29 Nordiska muséet ms N⁰ 41.674 Per Persson known as "Neringen." Johnson, *Svartkonstböcker*, 415. Lönsboda, Strömhult, Frostentorp, 1674, item N⁰ 11. Whilst the ms bears the date 1674, this may have been copied later. It is believed by his descendants to have been written by Persson who lived 1759–1834 in Lönsboda in Osby Parish in Northeast Skåne. Much of the rest of the ms is devoted to use the divining rod to discover treasure.

30 ms KUIII20 Svartkonstbok [Black Arts book] Slimminge socken, Vemmenhögs härad, Skåne, 1853 item N⁰ 60. Johnson, *Svartkonstböcker*, 281.

31 Johansson, Spells and Conjurations, item N⁰ 1 in ms c. Sometimes a knife with a black handle was

used to stir the liquor. Johnson, *Svartkonstböcker*, 332–33.

32 Arborén, Magic Book, item N⁰ 35. Johnson, *Svartkonstböcker*, 273.

33 Arborén, Magic Book, item N⁰ 22. Johnson, *Svartkonstböcker*, 271.

34 Erik Therman, *Bland noider och nomader* (Tammerfors-Tampere, 1940), 224, cited in Atrid Grimsson, *Svartkonstbok: Om shamanism, folklig läkekonst och magi* (Stockholm: Vattumannenförlag, 1992).

35 Arborén, Magic Book. item N⁰ 24. Johnson, *Svartkonstböcker*, 271.

36 KUIII20, Black Arts Book, item No. 82. Johnson, *Svartkonstböcker*, 285–86.

37 Nordiska muséet MS N⁰ 33.824 item N⁰ 55. Johnson, *Svartkonstböcker*, 365. In this charm, the mention of the altar of the church is enciphered.

38 Ahlström, Rademin, item N⁰ 53. Johnson, *Svartkonstböcker*, 246: "I conjure you, you spirit of the dead one's body, that you will drive the damned thief that stole from me N. N. so that he confesses; this publicly or carries it back again or Pain and Suffering for him until I shall order you in the name of F: S: the H: Gh: amen."

39 Ahlström, The Great Catechism, item 20. Johnson, *Svartkonstböcker*, 252.

40 Solomon's Magical Arts, item N⁰ 92. Johnson, *Svartkonstböcker*, 580.

41 C. O. Svahns Svartkonstbok [C. O. Swahn's Black

Arts Book,] C. O. Svahn, 1st Magic Professor Stockholm, item N⁰ 26. Johnson, *Svartkonstböcker*, 603: "Take earth from three cemeteries and put under the altar for three Sundays. When you have it in your shoes under your feet and walk around any animal, then it won't walk over your footprints. If you walk around a fire, then it will be contained within those bounds." Posited origin (based on dialect): Tveta socken, Aspelands län, Småland, handwriting appears to date from first half of the nineteenth century.

42 Swahn, Black Arts Book, item 6. Johnson, *Svartkonstböcker*, 601.

43 LUF. A. 795:26–31 Magiska formler och magiska handlingar Diversa anteckningar [Magical spells and magical procedures Diverse notes] Lunds universitets Folkminnessamling. Johnson, *Svartkonstböcker*, 428.

44 Halmdahl, The Key of Saint Peter, item N⁰ 12. Johnson, *Svartkonstböcker*, 307: To "lower" or suppress a girl. Take a nail from a grave and some dirt. Take it in all the names, put it into where a girl has peed while it is still warm, and say thereupon "Teeth and Tongue, Mouth and Bonedust." She's acquired this spell from "K."

45 Solomon's Magical Arts, item N⁰ 1. Johnson, *Svartkonstböcker*, 560–61. The reference to a "four-rimmed circle" with corners is enigmatic. One interpretation is that it may be a Saint John's Arms [⌘], which has a form that accentuates a

four-rimmed aspect. The glyph is protective, and in Sweden it has become the road sign indicating a preserved ancient monument. The fourfold nature of this charm stands out from the general emphasis upon the Trinity in the practice of the Wise Ones.

46 Nordiska muséet, MS unnumbered, Om fiskeri å des inehål [Regarding Fishing and its Equipage], item N⁰ 91. Johnson, *Svartkonstböcker*, 503. Handwriting of this manuscript suggests it originates from the late seventeenth to early eighteenth century.

47 Swahn, Black Arts Book, item N⁰ 81. Johnson, *Svartkonstböcker*, "So that birds can't fly outside a certain circle or terrain," 613.

48 Nordiska muséet, MS unnumbered, Att bota en bössa som är skämd, [To fix a shotgun that is hexed], item No. 20. Johnson, *Svartkonstböcker*, "A better and surer/safer way to come as close to a bird as one wants," 520.

49 Nordiska muséet, MS unnumbered 1. Att läsa mot värk—10. att förgöra en fiol" Gryts och Gåringe Skogsbygd, Södermanland, item N⁰ 6. Johnson, *Svartkonstböcker*, 475.

50 Nordiska muséet, MS unnumbered, Att bota en bössa som är skämd, [To fix a shotgun that is hexed], item N⁰ 21. Johnson, *Svartkonstböcker*, 520.

51 Leonhard Fredrik Rääf, K. Robert V. Wikman, ed., *Svenska Skrock och Signerier*. Kungliga Vitterhets Historie och Antikvitets Akademiens Handlingar,

Filologisk-filosofiska serien 4, (Stockholm: Almqvist & Wiksell, 1957), 141, N° 471.

52 Tillhagen, *Folklig Läkekonst*, 79. This lore being recorded in Jukkasjärvi, Lappland. Johnson, *Svartkonstböcker*, 603.

53 Eslöv #1 [EM 3329 A] "N° 1 Rademin: dätt är öfning i vettskapp ok konster", Denna boek tillhör mig B. I. Ahlström, item N° 35. Johnson, *Svartkonstböcker*, 243.

54 Svartkonstbok from Mo, Rådom, Västnorrlands län, Lapp land LU F, MSS A, B, C, Collection C. W. von Sydow, "II. Sendings," item N° 3. Johnson, *Svartkonstböcker*, 330-32.

55 Tillhagen, *Folklig Läkekonst*, 67. Collected in Holms parish, Medelpad. Compare Johnson, *Svartkonstböcker*, 331.

56 Nordiska muséet ms N° 271.600 15:1949 Konstbok [Book of Art] item N° 45. Johnson, *Svartkonstböcker*, 425: "To put the diarrhea on someone. Take a nail that has sat in a coffin. Nail it into his feces." A small bound ms, a little more than 4 inches tall. The cover is black, with the title picked out in white, an appearance particularly associated with the Black Art Books.

57 Folklore Society of Lund. *Varuti jag skrifver varjehanda* [*In which I write a bit of everything*] Petter Johan Johanesson, 1841, item N° 22. Johnson, *Svartkonstböcker*, 541-42. The MS being lodged with J. A. Sandblom, a teacher in Hultsjö. Of the MS, the author notes: "this book is to read in order to

learn many different types of wounds both to heal magically and other ways to learn to heal."
58 Johanesson, *Varuti jag skrifver varjehanda*, item Nº 45. Johnson, *Svartkonstböcker*, 545. A concluding addendum clarifies, "for this means, you borrow a human skull at a certain time during which you are planting the peas, and with the condition under the plant that no one can take from it except he will remain standing there and will leave it thereafter the appointed time, surely."
59 Tillhagen, *Folklig Läkekonst*, 81. Collected in Holms parish, Sköns parish, Medelpad.
60 Swahn, Black Arts Book, item Nº 93. Johnson, *Svartkonstböcker*, 615.
61 Erik Therman, *Bland noider och nomader* (Tammerfors-Tampere, 1940), 224, cited in Atrid Grimsson, *Svartkonstbok: Om shamanism, folklig läkekonst och magi* (Stockholm: Vattumannenförlag, 1992).
62 Tillhagen, *Folklig Läkekonst*, 79. Collected in Östra Frölunda, Västergötland.
63 Solomon's Magical Arts, item Nº 2. Johnson, *Svartkonstböcker*, 561.
64 Tillhagen, *Folklig Läkekonst*, 79. This lore being recorded in Jukkasjärvi, Lappland.
65 Solomon's Magical Arts, item Nº 98. Johnson, *Svartkonstböcker*, 561.
66 KUIII20, Svartkonstbok [Black Arts Book], Slimminge socken, Vemmenhögs härad, Skåne, 1853, item Nº 67. Johnson, *Svartkonstböcker*, 282.

67 Kulturhistoriska muséet in Härnösand, Cånster att bruka, nembligen: [Arts to employ, namely, Anders P., item N⁰ 1 in manuscript subtitled Black Arts of Anders P. Johnson, *Svartkonstböcker*, 223. Informed opinion dates the manuscript to the late eighteenth century, with internal evidence suggesting it is a copy made then of an earlier text.

68 Solomon's Magical Arts, item N⁰ 119. Johnson, *Svartkonstböcker*, 584. Given to Præpositus P. Starck by a traveller from Lappland to Karlskrona.

69 Johansson, Spells and Conjurations, item N⁰ 14 & an extract from N⁰ 1. Johnson, *Svartkonstböcker*, 333, 339.

70 Solomon's Magical Arts, *op cit.*, item N⁰ 71: "If you want so that no one will be able to steal from you when you are out on some journey." Johnson, *Svartkonstböcker*, 573–74.

71 Halmdahl, The Book of Healing, item N⁰ 136. Johnson, *Svartkonstböcker*, 458.

72 Necromantic/Nigromantic Matters, item N⁰ 4. Johnson, *Svartkonstböcker*, 466.

73 Solomon's Magical Arts, *op cit.*, item N⁰ 51. Johnson, *Svartkonstböcker*, 570.

74 Halmdahl, The Book of Healing, item N⁰ 72: "To get power in a knife." Johnson, *Svartkonstböcker*, 449. Halmdahl received this ritual from a Wise One whose name is abbreviated as Ol. Trac. in September 1936.

75 Solomon's Magical Arts, item N⁰ 3. Johnson, *Svartkonstböcker*, 561.

76 Swahn, Black Arts Book, item N⁰ 41. Johnson,

Svartkonstböcker, 606.
77 KU III20, Black Arts Book, item N⁰ 22: "If a shotgun is bewitched for you." Johnson, *Svartkonstböcker*, 276.
78 LUF. MS A. 285, Svartkonstbok från Glimåkra socken Skåne [Black arts book from Glimåkra parish, Skåne], Eva Wigström, 1870s, item N⁰ 4. Johnson, *Svartkonstböcker*, 301. The following note accompanies the MS: "The book in question, which was somewhat more detailed than what is recorded below, belonged to an 80 year old man, who died this past year in the vicinity of Broby, and was called "Skägelen" ("Little beard"). His father, who dwelt in Simonstorp, Glimåkra parish, was a so-called "Wise One" who owned the book in question, which is a manuscript from the 1700s."
79 Regarding Fishing and its Equipage, item N⁰ 45. Johnson, *Svartkonstböcker*, 497–98.
80 Solomon's Magical Arts, item N⁰ 3. Johnson, *Svartkonstböcker*, 582.
81 KUIII20, Black Arts Book, item N⁰ 117. Johnson, *Svartkonstböcker*, 291–92.
82 NM271.600 15:1949 Book of Art, item N⁰ 29. Johnson, *Svartkonstböcker*, 424.
83 KUIII20, Black Arts Book, item N⁰ 39. Johnson, *Svartkonstböcker*, 278.
84 Black Arts of Anders P., Härnösand, *op cit.*, N⁰ 52. Johnson, *Svartkonstböcker*, 231.
85 Swahn, Black Arts Book, item N⁰ 60. Johnson, *Svartkonstböcker*, 610.

86 Swahn, Black Arts Book, item N⁰ 59. Johnson, *Svartkonstböcker*, 609.
87 Ahlström, N⁰ 1; Rademin, item N⁰ 51. Johnson, *Svartkonstböcker*, 245.
88 Swahn, Black Arts Book, item N⁰ 66. Johnson, *Svartkonstböcker*, 610-11.
89 Solomon's Magical Arts, *op cit.*, item N⁰ 106. Johnson, *Svartkonstböcker*, 583.
90 Swahn, Black Arts Book, item N⁰ 62. Johnson, *Svartkonstböcker*, 610.
91 Swahn, Black Arts Book, item N⁰ 58. Johnson, *Svartkonstböcker*, 609.
92 Johansson, Spells and Conjurations, item N⁰ 3 in the supplement to MS C. Johnson, *Svartkonstböcker*, 329.
93 Solomon's Magical Arts, item N⁰ 58. Johnson, *Svartkonstböcker*, 571.
94 Johansson, Spells and Conjurations, item N⁰ 2 in the supplement to MS C: "To make oneself invisible. One takes [buys] a human bone on a Thursday night between twelve and one. On it, one scrapes with a knife, so that it becomes as flour. One takes this flour and strews it on the head as one says:

With this I disguise myself in an invisible way as a spirit, that at one time was united with this bone, and I leave my soul in pledge [as security]. Bornus Bister under the Devil's sigil in the name of God the Father and of the Son and of the Holy Ghost.

When one wants to once again become visible,

heave the knife into a tree, or a wall in the house."
Johnson, *Svartkonstböcker*, 329.
95 Necromantic/Nigromantic Matters, *op cit.*, item Nº 3. Johnson, *Svartkonstböcker*, 465-66.
96 VFF 2153, ss 1-3 G. Rodén uppt. G. Rodén, 1942,15/5 Munkfors, Ransäter sn., Värmland.
97 Solomon's Magical Arts, item Nº 73. Johnson, *Svartkonstböcker*, 574-76; also 465.
98 Johansson, Spells and Conjurations, unnumbered item appearing first item in MS C. Johnson, *Svartkonstböcker*, 327-29.
99 VFF 2153, ss 1-3 G. Rodén uppt. G. Rodén, 1942.
100 Johansson, Spells and Conjurations, item Nº 13. Johnson, *Svartkonstböcker*, 339.
101 Tillhagen, *Folklig Läkekonst*, 6-9.
102 NM 271.601 A-C, Halmdahl, Stockholm, 1929-39.
103 Bergstrand, *Trolldom och klokskap i Västergötland under 1800 talet*, 6.
104 Elisabet Dillner, "Lisa of Finshult and her 'Smöjträ,'" in Tillhagen, ed., *Papers on Folk-Medicine*, 118.
105 Tillhagen, *Folklig Läkekonst*, 136.
106 See *Johan J. Törners Samling af Widskeppelser, med inledning och anärkningar*. Edited by K. Robert V. Wikman, (Uppsala: Almqvist & Wiksell, 1946).

SELECT BIBLIOGRAPHY

Ankarloo, Bengt and Gustav Henningsen, eds. *Early Modern European Witchcraft: Centres and Peripheries*. Oxford: Oxford UP, 1990.

Bergstrand. Carl-Martin. *Trolldom och klokskap i Västergötland under 1800 talet.* Distribution, Borås: H. Borgströms bokhandel, 1932. Lund: Aktiebolaget Skånska Centraltryckeriet, 1932.

Davies, Owen. *Cunning Folk: Popular Magic in English History.* London: Hambledon and London, 2003.

―――. *Grimoires: A History of Magic Books.* Oxford: Oxford UP, 2009.

Dillner, Elisabet. "Lisa of Finshult and her 'Smöjträ,'" 117-31, in Carl-Herman Tillhagen, ed., *Papers on Folk-Medicine given at an Inter-Nordic Symposium at Nordiska Museet, Stockholm 8-10 May 1961*, Stockholm: Almqvist & Wiksell, 1963.

Edsman, Carl-Martin. "Folklig sed med rot i heden tid." *Arv* 1&2 (1946): 145-76.

―――. "Sjätte och sjunde Mosebok." *Saga och sed* (1962): 63-102.

―――. "Svartkonstböcker i sägen och historia." *Saga och sed* (1959): 160-68.

Linderholm, Emanuel. "Signelser och besvärjelser från medeltid och nytid." *Svenska landsmål och svenskt folkliv* 41 (1927, -29, -39): 1-478.

Peuckert, Will-Erich. "Die Ägyptischen Geheimnisse."
    Arv 10 (1954): 40-96.
Rääf, Leonhard Fredrik., K. Robert V. Wikman, ed. *Svenska Skrock och Signerier*. Kungliga Vitterhets Historie och Antikvitets Akademiens Handlingar, Filologiskfilosofiska serien 4. Stockholm: Almqvist & Wiksell, 1957.
Tillhagen, Carl-Herman. *Folklig Läkekonst*. Stockholm: Nordiska Muséet. 1958.
von Sydow, C. W. "Det ovanligas betydelse i tro och sed." *Folkminnen och folktankar* XIII (1926): 23 ff.
Wikman, K. Robert V., ed., *Johan J. Törners Samling af Widskeppelser, med inledning och anärkningar*. Skrifter utgivna av Kungl. Gustav Adolfs Akademien. 15. Uppsala: Almqvist & Wiksell, 1946.

THE GRAVEYARD WANDERS WAS TYPESET
BY JOSEPH UCCELLO USING AYER
POSTER BLACKLETTER, AYER POSTER,
STANLEY, ELIZA, MEDIA 77, PX GROTESK,
NEXT BOOK AND NEXT POSTER.

www.ingramcontent.com/pod-product-compliance
Lightning Source LLC
Chambersburg PA
CBHW030333100526
44592CB00010B/687